Don't Forget Your Shield!

Protection from the World's Influences

20 Short Stories

by
Jeff D. Chapman

xulon
PRESS

Don't Forget Your Shield!
by Jeff D. Chapman

Printed in the United States of America

ISBN 9781619960299

www.xulonpress.com

To my wife, Cassie, I am grateful for your
support and willingness to always modify your
schedule in order to allot me the time
necessary to complete the book.
To my children, Cade and Seth, who provided me with
inspiration to write the book.
To my great friend, Jeff Sandifer, for all of the
advice and encouragement given from
start to finish.
To Linda Palmer, thanks for your many
contributions, editorial help,
honest feedback, and creativity.

Table of Contents

Guidelines for Effective Use of This Book

This book was written for young people and their parents in hopes that they would read the chapters and find truths applicable to their lives. Parents, if this material is beyond your child's reading level, you may want to read the stories aloud and then discuss the *Ask Yourself* and *Last Word* sections at the end of each.

Chapter One

SHOWING LOVE FOR OTHERS

Verse: A new command I give you. Love one another as I have loved you so you must love one another. By this all men will know that you are my disciples if you love one another.

John 13: 34-35

Can You Spare A Dime?

"Have a great day guys!" Bentley's mother brought her car to a stop next to the school gym and turned to the back seat. "And try to stay out of trouble."

McCall flashed an innocent smile. "Trouble? You know that Bentley and I *always* follow the rules."

The two boys could not keep straight faces and began to snicker.

"Oh, of course you do," replied Bentley's mother, pretending to agree with McCall. "So I must have just imagined the call I received from the principal's office last year?"

"Mom, that was just a misunderstanding," Bentley pointed out as he began to exit the car. "McCall and I are doing a lot better this year."

"Well, keep up the good work," she said just as the car door closed. The two boys laughed as they made their way down the sidewalk.

"Your mom will never let us forget about our visit to the principal's office, will she?" McCall asked.

"Probably not. At least she's now able to joke about it."

McCall didn't hear Bentley. Something else had captured his attention. "Look over there." He pointed at a lady walking through the parking lot. "The meanest teacher in the entire school, Miss Thetus."

"I don't know about her being mean, but she does give us a lot of homework," said Bentley.

"Oh, look! She just dropped her papers, and the wind is blowing them all over the parking lot. That's hilarious!"

Without hesitation, Bentley raced across the parking lot to his teacher and began to assist her. McCall looked on in disbelief as Bentley chased down papers flying in every direction. Within seconds, Bentley returned the papers to Miss Thetus and hurried back to his friend.

As Bentley approached, McCall shook his head in disgust. "What was that all about?"

"What do you mean?"

"Why did you help her?" asked McCall. "Better yet, why would *anyone* want to help her?"

"It's just the right thing to do. I hope someone would help me if *my* papers were flying around everywhere."

McCall shook his head in bewilderment as they entered the school building. Once inside, the two boys could barely hear their own voices. The school's main entrance was busy and full of life. Students rushed up and down the hall while many others chatted loudly along the long rows of lockers.

As Bentley and McCall dodged oncoming traffic, Bentley yelled, "It's loud in here. Let's go hang out at the playground."

Suddenly, there was a tugging on Bentley's shirt just as he began to make his way down the long hallway. He whirled around to see a much younger student trying to get his attention.

"Hi, Bentley," the younger boy said sheepishly.

Bentley nodded a greeting. "Oh, hi, Brian. What's going on?"

"Well, uh, I have a math test right after second recess and don't think I, uh, really know how to do it." Brian flushed. "I was wondering if, uh, you, uh, might have time to show me how to do it...since you're so good at math and all." He timidly looked down at the floor as he awaited Bentley's response.

"Sure, I can help you." Bentley dropped to a knee in order to make direct eye contact with the young student. "Meet me back here at recess, and don't forget to bring your math book, okay?"

"Thanks!" exclaimed Brian, beaming. "See you later."

As he departed, McCall approached, frowning. "What were you doing? I was at the end of the hall thinking you'd followed me, and then I find you talking with some little kid."

Bentley smiled. "Oh, I know him. We go to the same church. I agreed to help him get ready for his math test at recess."

McCall stepped back. "Are you kidding? Remember, Toby and Patrick challenged us to a basketball game at recess. If we back out, they'll say we're scared."

"I'm not worried about what Toby and Patrick will say. We can play ball with them anytime. Brian's test is *today*."

As McCall shook his head in dismay, Bentley resumed making his way down the hallway. "I just don't understand you sometimes," McCall mumbled as he followed his friend.

The two boys weaved their way to the end of the hallway. Bentley pushed against the double doors leading outside, but they thudded instead of swinging open. He quickly realized that something was blocking them. Cracking the doors open, Bentley peered through the small opening. He could see a student in a wheelchair just outside. They forced the door

11

open a few more inches and managed to squeeze through. There they recognized the student.

"Hey, Benny, what's going on?" McCall asked.

Benny appeared upset as he pointed at the wheelchair ramp. "I'm stuck here because all of those backpacks are blocking my way down the ramp."

Before Benny could ask for help, Bentley and McCall leapt from the ramp to the ground and began the process of removing backpacks, making a clear path for the wheelchair. In no time, Benny was able to make his way to the bottom of the ramp to join his friends.

"Thanks, guys," he said with a grin and a wave.

"No problem," said McCall.

The three boys talked and joked around until the bell sounded for school to begin.

Later in the library

McCall occupied his time at a magazine rack while Bentley checked out a book on science projects. Once finished, Bentley sat down at a nearby table. Seeing this, McCall grabbed a magazine and joined his friend. As McCall sat down, something captured his attention at the librarian's desk. This did not go unnoticed by Bentley, who turned in his chair to see what he was looking at.

"It's Clint," McCall whispered. "I can't stand him. He's always bragging on himself, especially about how his baseball team won the championship."

Bentley agreed with a nod. "He doesn't seem very nice. Last week, he told the teacher that I cut in front of him in the lunch line, *and I didn't*."

"That sounds like him," McCall said.

"Well, let's just ignore him." Bentley returned to his book.

McCall continued to watch Clint despite Bentley's suggestion. McCall could tell that Clint was not pleased with

Miss Ferrand, the school librarian. Due to the quietness of the room, McCall heard most of their discussion.

"You've had six weeks to pay your library fines, and we've given you many reminders," said Miss Ferrand. "You know the school rule, Clint. If you haven't paid your fines within six weeks, you spend recess in detention until you do."

Clint frowned. "But I only brought two dollars."

"I'm sorry, but that's no excuse. For weeks, I've told you exactly what you owe. Last Friday, I recall you laughing at me and not taking my words seriously."

McCall began to smile and leaned closer to Bentley. "Hey, are you getting this?"

Bentley looked up from his book. "No, uh, I was reading."

"Clint is going to get detention because he's a dime short on paying his library fine."

Bentley shifted in his chair to see Clint pleading his case to Miss Ferrand. He then turned back to McCall. "So you say Clint's a dime short, huh?" He reached into a pocket of his jacket.

"Hey, Clint!" Bentley's shout startled those sitting around him. "Catch!"

Already in a bad mood, Clint scowled as he turned to see what Bentley was up to. At that moment, Bentley hurled what he'd taken from his pocket in Clint's direction. Clint instinctively caught the object to avoid being smacked in the head. Angrily, he looked down to see what it was. His expression instantly changed from anger to confusion as he stared at the dime resting in the palm of his hand. Speechless, Clint looked up at Bentley. "Uh, thanks man." He handed the dime to Miss Ferrand.

Miss Ferrand smiled. "You're lucky to have a friend like Bentley. Because of his good deed, you've escaped detention."

Still shocked, Clint didn't know what to say for a few seconds. "Yes, ma'am," he finally replied, turning to leave.

He cut his eyes towards Bentley as he passed. As their eyes met, Clint quickly looked away in embarrassment, undoubtedly remembering how he'd treated Bentley a week ago.

"Are you crazy?" McCall said. "Why did you help him after he lied and got you into trouble?"

Bentley grinned. "My Uncle Audy has always told me 'do unto others as you would have them do unto you.'"

"What exactly does that mean?"

"It means that you should treat people the way that you want them to treat you."

"But what if they aren't nice to me even when I'm nice to them?"

"Don't worry so much about how *others* choose to act," Bentley said. "You have no control over that. Try to be more concerned about how God wants *you* to act."

McCall didn't immediately reply. He appeared to be in deep thought. After a few moments, he began smiling. "Oh, I see. That's why you were nice to Miss Thetus this morning in the parking lot and why you helped that kid with his math. Then you helped Benny at the wheelchair ramp. And last but not least, it's why you kept Clint out of detention."

"That's right," said Bentley. "These are the kind of little things that I can do each day to show a caring attitude. This is what God wants *all* of us to do. And if you look around, you'll see chances to show love for others too."

"Well, maybe I'll give it a try," replied McCall as he playfully slapped his friend on the back.

Bentley grinned. "Believe me, it's worth it. You'll make people around you happier, and you'll be happier too."

"Sounds good to me!"

Ask Yourself...

1. Ways of "showing love for others" includes being kind and helpful. Do you consider yourself to be a kind and helpful person most of the time? Explain.

2. Why is it important to "show love for others"?

3. Can you identify three ways you can show that you are one of God's disciples through helping others? List each.

Last Word

In our story's verse, God commands us to love one another. If God commands something, it has to be important. So, why is it important?

First of all, God showed us a great example of love by sending his own Son, Jesus, to die a horrible death on a cross so we could be forgiven for our sins. Just think, God loves us so much that he allowed his Son to die for us! This should make it easy to see why God expects us to show love for one another. Is God asking too much from us? Certainly not.

Okay, let's say that you "love others." The next important step is to make sure that people know that you feel love for them. This is important because it will help others to see that you follow God and his teachings. People will be able to see God in you through your actions. This may even assist others in becoming a Christian, which would be *awesome*. Anyway, if you look around, it doesn't take long to figure out ways to show love. Consider Bentley in our story. He showed love by performing many kind acts at school, even once for a person that he didn't get along with. Over time, others will take notice of these kind acts, much like McCall did in our story. Showing love will help you to build friendships, have less conflict in your life, and most importantly, it's pleasing to God. Give it a try starting today!

Chapter Two

DEALING WITH OPPOSITION

Verse: If God is for us, who can be against us?

Romans 8:31

Dare To Be Different

"All right, students, let's get started," Miss Coon said as she brought her class to attention. "This morning is the deadline for turning in permission slips for our spring field trip. If you have one, please pass it to the front of your row."

As she collected permission slips, someone knocked on the door. Students watched curiously as Miss Coon walked over and welcomed in Principal Stobaugh and a girl that they did not recognize. The girl was extremely tall and had long blonde hair. The class continued to watch as the pair spoke with Miss Coon in hushed tones. After a few moments, the three turned to face the class.

Principal Stobaugh spoke first. "Good morning, class. I'm pleased to announce that we have a new student today." He gestured towards the girl. "Her name is Eliza, and I know that all of you will do your part to make her feel welcome. Eliza, would you like to take a moment to tell the class a little about yourself?"

"Sure." Eliza stepped forward. "As Principal Stobaugh

said, my name is Eliza, and I'm from a small town in northern California. We moved here to be closer to my grandmother. She's been sick a lot lately. I have one sister named Mary. Let's see…I love sports, probably the high jump is my favorite. I also like playing the cello. I'm happy to be here and hope to meet all of you soon." Eliza smiled as she stepped back, indicating that she had finished her introduction.

"You're a very interesting girl," said Miss Coon. "Take any unoccupied desk and let's get started."

After Miss Coon's Class

"Oh my gosh! Did you all see how tall the new girl is?" asked Melissa.

Angie laughed. "How could I not? She was as tall as Principal Stobaugh."

"Yeah, but what was that weird talk about liking the high jump?" asked Patsy. "We don't even have that at our school. Surely she plays basketball."

Angie shrugged. "All I know is that we already have a good basketball team. With her, I bet we'd be fantastic."

Melissa nodded. "At recess, we'll definitely have a talk with her about joining the team. You all know that I can be very persuasive." She snickered.

Patsy glanced down at her watch. "Oh, guys, we better hurry if we're going to get to the library on time."

Without hesitation, the three girls grabbed their books and hurried down the hallway.

Recess

"You seem very different than most of the students at this school," Nikki said to Eliza, quickly adding, "I mean that in a good way!"

"It's okay." Eliza laughed as they made their way through

the busy schoolyard. "My parents have always taught me to just be myself, so I don't mind being a little different."

"That's cool. I've just never met anyone who likes the cello, the high jump, art, and deep sea fishing."

Eliza laughed again. "I guess I'm lucky to have parents that have given me a chance to try a lot of different things."

"How about over there?" Nikki asked as she pointed to a vacant picnic table. "That's a good place to sit."

As the two walked over and sat atop the picnic table, Eliza checked out her new and unfamiliar surroundings. Scanning the schoolyard, she noticed three girls who appeared to be staring at her. Eliza looked away from them. "Nikki, who are those girls sitting on the bench to your left? I feel like they've been watching me all day. Do you know them?"

Nikki glanced in their direction and quickly looked away, hoping the girls didn't suspect that they were being discussed. She lowered her voice. "That's Melissa, Patsy, and Angie. They're the best basketball players in the school and probably the most popular."

"I wonder why they've been staring at me."

"They're probably just curious because you're our newest student."

"Maybe."

Nikki's face brightened. "Hey, I'm about to get a candy bar and something to drink. Do you want anything?"

"Could you get me a bottled water? I'll pay you when you get back."

"Consider it a gift for a new student on her first day." Grinning, Nikki left.

"Nikki seems so nice. I believe I've already made a new friend." Eliza reached into her backpack and grabbed her class schedule. As she studied over it, she realized that she wasn't alone and quickly looked up. To her surprise, the three girls that had been staring stood before her. Startled, Eliza fumbled through yet another introduction. "H-hi girls.

19

I'm Eliza. I don't think we've met."

"I'm Melissa and this is Angie and Patsy," said one of them.

Eliza felt uncomfortable, wondering why they'd approached her. They didn't seem overly friendly and hadn't even cracked a smile. Eliza forced her own smile to possibly lighten the mood. "So, are you girls in any of my classes?"

"Yeah," replied Melissa. "We're all in your English class."

"Oh, okay."

Angie cleared her throat. "We heard you tell the class—"

Melissa turned sharply and glared at her friend, who instantly stopped speaking and looked down at the ground. Turning back to Eliza, Melissa faked a smile. "I think what Angie was going to say is that we heard you mention that the high jump was your favorite sport. I know you're new here and all, but we don't do the high jump at this school. At our school, girls only play basketball, softball, and volleyball."

Eliza gave them a thoughtful smile. "Oh, I know there haven't been any high jumpers at this school, but that may soon change. My dad is a high jump coach and has offered to help any kids interested in learning how to do it. Principal Stobaugh said that we can even form a team and compete against other schools."

Melissa clearly hadn't expected that response, which left her stammering. "I-I don't think anyone will really care about the high jump. Basketball rules at this school."

Eliza pretended not to notice Melissa's negative statement. "You may be right. I guess we'll see."

Melissa took a step closer, which made Eliza more uncomfortable. "You know, there's no doubt that the basketball players are the most popular here at this school. Patsy, Angie, and I would like to invite you to be a part of our team and enjoy all of the benefits that come with it."

Eliza was confused. "Why do you want me on your team?"

Melissa laughed. "Isn't it obvious? You're the tallest girl in the entire school! You're our one missing piece. With you, we'll win the championship."

"Sorry, guys, but I really don't like playing basketball. Besides, I don't think I'm really that good at it."

"Yeah, right," Patsy retorted. "How hard could it be for you? You're so tall, you can probably just drop the ball in the hoop."

Eliza knew she had to be clear. These girls had no intentions of taking no for an answer. "Thanks for asking, but I'm not interested in playing basketball."

Melissa's cheeks flushed. She was obviously not used to being turned down by anyone. Hands on her hips, she moved even closer to Eliza before speaking, which put them face to face. "I don't think you understand. If you join us, people will like you at this school. If you refuse to join the team, we can make your time at this school very unpleasant."

Though Eliza found Melissa's words hurtful, she made her best effort not to appear upset. "It sounds like you'll only be my friend if I do what you say. I want friends that like me for who I am and realize that I can think for myself."

Melissa's eyes widened. She could not believe that Eliza had stood up to her. She turned to her two sidekicks. "Let's go. She'll be sorry!"

As the three girls stormed off, Eliza realized that her heart was racing and her palms were sweating. She took a deep breath. *I thought they would never leave.*

At Eliza's house after school

"Hm. Sounds like you had an interesting first day." Eliza's father leaned back in his rocking chair. "I know that you have some concerns about the three girls on the basketball team, but you need to also remember that good things happened at school today."

"I know, I know." Eliza shrugged. "It's just that Melissa's said I'd 'be sorry.' I can't help but think about that."

Eliza's mother shook her head. "Try not to worry. Remember, you aren't responsible for anyone's behavior but your own. Just try to focus on the things *you* can control."

Eliza's father nodded. "I want you to know that your mom and I are really proud of how you handled those girls. We like how you stood up for yourself and also controlled your temper."

"That's not always an easy thing to do," Eliza's mother added.

Eliza smiled. "I just tried to do what you've taught me. When they threatened me, I remembered that God was with me. That gave me strength."

"That's right," Eliza's father told her. "When I feel like someone is against me, I say a little prayer. It helps me to deal with these types of situations better. Hey, how can I lose with God as my partner twenty-four hours a day? I tell you, it makes my problems seem a whole lot smaller!"

Eliza gave them a big smile. "That's a good way to think about it. Anyway, I also had some good moments at school. I'm not going to let one bad thing ruin my entire day."

"That's what I like to hear!" Eliza's mother exclaimed. "What do you say we all go to town for ice cream to celebrate a successful first day?"

Eliza leaped from the couch. "That's what *I* like to hear!" She purposefully echoed her mother's words. "What are we waiting for? Let's go!"

Ask Yourself...

1. Have you ever felt like someone was against you? If so, how did you react?

2. Consider your reaction to opposition. Do you think it was pleasing to God? Explain.

3. Our verse states, "If God is for us, who can be against us?" How did Eliza benefit from fully understanding this?

Last Word

In our story, it didn't take long for Eliza to have three students against her. It was only her first day of school! To make matters worse, Eliza did absolutely nothing wrong. Unfortunately, situations like Eliza's cannot be avoided. No matter what you do or how hard you try to avoid conflict, sooner or later someone will surely be "against" you. It happens to everyone.

Since we have established that there will be times that you experience conflict, it only makes sense to be ready. Our verse states, "If God is for us, who can be against us?" Understanding that God is with you at all times (especially during conflict) can give you great strength during these difficult moments. Eliza kept in mind that God was with her. This was much more important to her than the fact that three girls were against her.

Having God as the center of your life results in great reward, much more than any human being can give you. Through God, you will greatly improve your ability to get through times when you face opposition.

Chapter Three

GIVING YOUR BEST EFFORT

Verse: Whatever your hands find to do, do it with all your might.

Ecclesiastes 9:10

Easy Street

"All right, class. That wraps up our chapter on atoms so please put away your science books," Miss Saint said. "I have an announcement to make." She paused until the rustling of books and papers could no longer be heard. "It's time for those interested in our Lab Buddies competition to choose a partner and get signed up."

A student raised her hand.

"Yes, Debbie, do you have a question?"

"Will we have the same rules as last year?"

Miss Saint nodded. "For the most part. Each team will require one partner to be tested in math and the other in science. The best team score will be recognized as the 'School Champion' of your grade level."

"Can we choose any partner we want?" questioned Garret, who did not raise his hand.

Miss Saint sighed. "Yes, Garret. You can choose anyone you want as long as they are in the same grade that you're in."

"Okay everyone, I want to make it official that Griffin and I will be partners again this year." As the two boys exchanged high fives, the rest of the students groaned loudly in protest.

"That's not fair!" cried Debbie. "The two smartest kids in science and math shouldn't be a team. That means that no one else has a chance to win."

Soon, many other students joined Debbie in opposing the boys' partnership. Garret and Griffin smiled broadly as they listened to a multitude of objections and complaints from their classmates.

Finally, Miss Saint stepped in. "Class, that's enough! If Garret and Griffin choose to be Lab Buddies, it's perfectly fine and within the rules. There's something each of you need to decide right now. Are you going to accept defeat without even trying or will you choose to put in the work necessary to win? We're offering one-hour classes each day after school to better prepare you for the science and math testing. I encourage all of you to take advantage of these classes."

In the back of the classroom, Paige nudged her friend, Andra. "What do you say we become partners and give it a try?"

"Do you think we'd have a chance to win?" asked Andra.

"We'll never know unless we try."

Andra hesitated momentarily as she considered the invitation. "Oh sure, why not?" She smiled. "When do you want to start preparing?"

"As soon as possible. I think that maybe we should try to make the classes each day after school to make sure we're ready for the contest."

"Sounds good!" Andra grinned as she shook Paige's hand.

One Week Later

"Garret, it's time to stop playing video games and start doing your homework!" his mother yelled from down the hall.

"Oh, all right," Garret moaned as he looked at Griffin. "I was hoping we'd have time to play one more game. We've been getting really close to our high score."

"Ahh, that's okay," Griffin replied as he got up off the floor. "I've got to get home anyway. We can go for the high score tomorrow."

Garret nodded as his friend exited the bedroom. When Griffin reached the doorway, he abruptly stopped. "Hey, I forgot to ask you something. Do you think we should go to some of those Lab Buddy classes after school to get ready for the contest?"

"Are you kidding? We don't need those classes." Garret laughed. "We always make the best grades, not to mention that we won the contest last year without even trying. Why waste our time studying any more than we already have to?"

"I, uh, guess you're right," stammered Griffin.

"Besides, all we really get for winning is a certificate and maybe our names in the newspaper."

"That's true." Griffin smiled. "Forget I even asked. I'll see you in the morning."

Six Days Later

"Is your mom supposed to be late today?" asked Andra, glancing at her watch. She and Paige had just finished their Lab Buddy class.

"Yeah, but only a few minutes." Paige scanned the school parking lot. "Before picking us up, she had to drop off Nanci at art class."

Andra nodded. "No big deal. I'm in no hurry."

"Actually, the extra time gives us one final chance to go over our strategy for Lab Buddies tomorrow morning."

"Good thinking," replied Andra. "So we agree that I'm testing in math while you take on the science section, right?"

"Well, you seem to be better at math, so I really think my focus should be on science."

Andra nodded again. "That's fine. Tonight, I'll take one last look at Chapter 12 in my math book. Oh, and remember that Miss Saint suggested that everyone taking the science test should review the questions on the solar system one last time."

"Don't worry, I'll remember," Paige assured her.

There was a thoughtful pause before Andra spoke again. "You know, we didn't miss even one class after school to get ready for this contest. Do you think we have a chance to win?"

"Oh, I definitely believe we have a chance to win, but I'm not even worried about it."

Andra couldn't believe her ears. "Not worried? I thought this was important to you."

Paige gave her a calm smile. "Lab Buddies *is* important to me, and I really *do* want to win, but I'm already satisfied because I know we've tried our best. My dad once told me that as long as I give my best effort, I should be proud."

"Hmm. I've never looked at it that way before. I'll try not to worry about it either."

"Good." Paige nodded enthusiastically. "And by the way, did you notice that Garret and Griffin didn't come to *any* of the after school classes?"

"I *did* notice that. Do you think that improves our chances to win?"

"Well, it doesn't hurt them," Paige said with a soft laugh.

"Oh, there's your mom!" Andra motioned to an approaching vehicle. The two girls hurried over to the car and soon were on their way.

Four Days Later

"All right guys, break time is over. Please take your seats," Miss Saint instructed her class. She waited patiently as students ended conversations and slowly made it back to their desks. As soon as the final student was seated, she spoke. "I have some exciting news. I have the results of Saturday's Lab Buddy competition."

This immediately created a buzz of excitement. The classroom noise level rose as students speculated over which team had won. "Class! Class!" shouted Miss Saint to settle them down. "I need everyone's attention so I can let you all know who won."

The classroom hushed as Miss Saint removed two red ribbons and then two blue ribbons from a folder on her desk. She placed the red ribbons on her desk while the blue ribbons remained in her hand.

Miss Saint smiled. "I'm pleased to announce that the winners of this year's Lab Buddy competition are…Paige and Andra!"

Amid a mixture of gasps and cheers, the two girls made their way to the front of the classroom. They beamed with joy as they accepted their awards. Garret, slumped in his desk, showed little reaction as he glanced over at Griffin. It was obvious that Griffin was unhappy.

"I knew we should have studied like everyone else!" Griffin snapped. "If we'd tried harder, *we* would've won."

"What's it really matter?" Garret responded. "All you get is a ribbon."

Griffin looked away in disgust.

Miss Saint again turned to the class.

"We also want to recognize our second place team." She picked up the red ribbons. "This year's second place winners are Griffin and Garret! Come on up here and join us."

The class clapped politely as the two boys slowly joined Paige and Andra. Miss Saint gave each boy a red ribbon. Garret and Griffin accepted their prize, then hastily returned to their desks.

Miss Saint again focused on the class. "I have a very special announcement to make, and I would like for Paige and Andra to remain up here with me for a moment."

The two girls had no problem remaining in front of the classroom. They were clearly enjoying the attention.

"This year, the Lab Buddy competition does not end here at our school. First place winners of each school will be heading to regional competition in Chicago. While there, Paige and Andra will not only compete in regional competition, but will also be treated with a tour of two science museums, a boat tour along Lake Michigan, and will even go to a professional baseball game. Congratulations, girls!"

The two girls squealed with excitement as the class cheered them on.

"I can't believe this," said Andra. "It's too good to be true!'

"Our hard work paid off." Paige hugged her friend.

The reaction was much different from Garret. He raised his hand, attempting to get Miss Saint's attention.

Finally, she spotted him. "Yes, Garret?"

"Are you saying that second place doesn't get anything but this ribbon?"

"I'm sorry," answered Miss Saint, "But regional competition only includes teams that scored the highest at each school."

"Well, Garret and I came in first place last year, and we didn't get to go to Chicago," interjected Griffin. "That's not fair."

"Well, Lab Buddies is only in its third year, and this is the first time they've had the funds to offer regional competition. Maybe you guys will win next year."

Garret and Griffin had little else to say. They spend the rest of the day considering how much fun they would've had together in Chicago. They spent a longer period of time regretting that they had not given their best effort.

Ask Yourself...

1. Can you identify a task or activity that you always give your best effort? Explain what makes you try so hard.

2. Can you identify a task or activity that you do not give your best effort? Explain why you have chosen not to try your best.

3. What are two benefits of giving your best effort?

Last Word

On an average day, we perform many tasks and activities. These may include basketball practice, studying for a test, or simply completing chores. Each time you perform a task or take part in an activity, you have a decision to make. You must decide if you're going to do your very best, giving your greatest effort. Or will you do just enough to get by? Unfortunately, many of us often choose not to give our best effort. We simply take the easiest path.

Based on our story's scripture, God clearly expects our best efforts in whatever we are doing. Why is this important to God? God has blessed us with abilities, and he expects us to always use them in a manner that shows that we appreciate the gifts that He has given. A lack of effort reveals that we are not grateful for what God gives us.

There is great reward in always choosing to do your best. For example, giving your best effort at basketball practice will make you a better basketball player. Studying hard will improve your grades. Even giving your best effort as you perform chores is rewarding. It pleases your parents, and that can be a really good thing! As Paige pointed out in our story, when you do your best, you should feel proud of yourself no matter what the result is.

There are benefits to giving your best effort on a regular basis. Those that choose to do so often develop into more confident people, and they also improve their chances of having good things happen in their lives.

It's also important to remember that choosing not to give your greatest effort has consequences. Just look at Garret and Griffin in our story. They had an excellent chance of winning the contest, but they chose not to give their best effort, and later regretted it. Do not make the same mistake as Garret and Griffin. Every single day, you have many opportunities to make the right choice. Do your best!

Chapter Four

FORGIVING

Verse: Forgive us our sins, for we also forgive everyone who sins against us. And lead us not into temptation.

Luke 11:4

Rock On?

"Mom, are you home?" Carter shouted as she burst through the front door. There was no response. She dropped her backpack on the living room table and looked around. A light was on in the hallway, and she could detect the sound of her mother's exercise video coming from the back bedroom.

"She's here!" Carter smiled broadly as she dashed down the hallway, practically flying into her mother's bedroom. Carter's mother, standing near the flung open door, screamed out of fright as her daughter rushed in. Surprised by her mother's reaction, Carter also began yelling. As they realized the situation, their screams quickly changed to laughter.

"Have you ever heard of knocking?" her mother asked, gasping for breath.

"But I have some exciting news that can't wait!"

Mom smiled. "Something tells me that I may not want to hear this."

Carter placed her hands on her hips. "Don't worry. It's

nothing crazy *this* time."

Carter's mother shook her head. "Okay, let me hear it."

"You know my friend, Kambree? She has four tickets to the Gina Giants concert, *and she asked me to go*! You know they're my absolute favorite band! *I can't believe it!*"

Carter's mother did not share in her daughter's excitement. "Who else is going?"

"Don't worry. Kambree's mom, Phyllis, is going. Kendra is invited too."

Carter's mother breathed a sigh of relief before continuing. "Isn't this concert only two days away? You do realize that I'll have to speak with Kambree's mother before you can go, right?"

"She'll be calling you tonight."

Mom smiled. "Okay, sounds good. I know you'll have a great time."

Next morning at school

As Carter entered the classroom, she had one single purpose: find Kambree. Last night, the excitement of the concert faded away as Carter waited and waited by the phone for her invitation. The call from Kambree never came. To say the least, Carter had a lot of questions.

"Carter!" yelled a voice from the back of the classroom.

Carter immediately recognized the voice of her friend, Kendra, who motioned Carter over to her desk. She didn't hesitate, hoping Kendra would have answers. As she approached, it was obvious to her that Kendra was upset. Her face was red, and she was frowning.

"Kambree didn't call me about the concert last night," said Kendra. "Did she call you?"

"No, and I really don't understand it. She said that we'd get a call with all of the details."

"Well, it's time for us to get some answers. Look who just

walked in." Carter had difficulty keeping up with Kendra, as she made a beeline to where Kambree was emptying her backpack.

Carter realized that Kendra was too angry to have a conversation without showing her temper. "Let me do the talking, okay?"

"Sure, whatever," snapped Kendra.

Kambree's back was to the girls.

"Hi, Kambree," Carter said softly.

Despite Carter's low tone, it startled Kambree. She jumped as she turned to face them. "Oh, uh, hi. Wh-what are you t-two doing?" Kambree seemed nervous.

It was already obvious to Carter that something was wrong. She could tell that Kambree was forcing a smile and that she could hardly make eye contact. Carter made a point to appear calm and pleasant. "Well, we didn't hear from you last night. We're wondering about the concert."

"Well, I, uh, kinda got some bad news." Kambree stared at the floor instead of meeting their gazes.

"What do you mean, bad news?" Kendra asked.

Kambree didn't look up. "Well, uh, my dad's boss at work promised us four tickets, but he, uh, ended up giving two tickets to his niece. So he only had two left, one for me and one for my mom."

Carter sagged with disappointment. "Bummer. I guess you can't help it, though—"

"It would've been nice to hear this from you last night!" yelled Kendra. "And you shouldn't have promised us tickets that you didn't even have! You had me so excited. Thanks for nothing."

"That's enough, girls," said Miss DeLaughter, their teacher. "Everyone, take a seat."

Carter quickly made her way to her desk. The disappointing news made it difficult for her to focus on her schoolwork. The longer that Carter thought about the concert, the more she felt anger instead of disappointment. Carter decided that she would have a talk with her mother after school. *Sometimes Mom knows just what to say when stuff like this happens*.

Later at Carter's Home

"So let me get this straight," Carter's mother said, making sure she understood her daughter's feelings. "You and Kendra are angry at Kambree because her dad's boss gave her only two tickets instead of four."

Carter attempted to hide her sheepish grin. "No, Mom. We're mad at Kambree because she promised to take us to the concert."

"All right, maybe it was wrong that she promised you a ticket before she actually had one. And maybe Kambree should've called you with the bad news last night. But I'm sure she was scared to tell you, knowing you'd be upset with her."

"But does that make it okay?"

"No, it doesn't. But I think you need to take a second and try to put yourself in Kambree's position."

Carter thought about her mother's words. After a moment, she spoke. "All right, mom. What do I need to do?"

"You need to get rid of the anger you're feeling towards Kambree."

"You make it sound so easy. How do I do that?"

"Forgive Kambree and move on. After all, we all make mistakes from time to time, don't we?"

Head lowered, Carter nodded. "I know you're right, Mom. It's just that I want to go to the concert so badly. It seemed too good to be true . . . and I guess it was."

Her mother nodded. "Right now you're thinking more about yourself. Once you are able to consider Kambree and her feelings, forgiveness will not be so hard."

Carter looked up. "I suppose you're right, Mom."

Her mother placed her arm around her daughter. "Carter, something I think about when I have trouble forgiving is to consider how God continues to forgive me for my sins every single day. Who am I not to forgive when God has chosen to keep forgiving me?"

Carter smiled. "That's a good point, Mom. I'm going to forgive Kambree. Anyway, I know she didn't want to hurt me."

"Once you do, you'll both feel better."

"Thanks, mom," whispered Carter.

Three months later

"Kambree, your family's camp is so cool," said Carter. "I wish my family had something like this."

Kambree grinned. "Thanks. Every year we spend the first two weeks of June here."

"I can't believe how much there is to do. Let's see, so far we've been fishing, hiking, swimming, and I've even learned to water ski!"

"And remember, tomorrow we're going to the water park."

Carter nodded. "I know. It's all been great. Thanks so much for inviting me."

"Hey, I really want to thank you too."

Carter was confused. "Thank me? For what?"

"For not holding a grudge and for forgiving me when I couldn't take you to the Gina Giants concert."

Carter smiled. "Don't worry about it. One of these days you may need to forgive me for something."

Kambree laughed. "You could be right about that."

"With a little help from my mom, I realized that forgiving was actually the easier choice. If I had chosen not to show forgiveness, I would've gone around angry all of the time, much like Kendra. Forgiving has given me a peaceful feeling and a special friend in you."

Kambree took a deep breath. "Do you think Kendra will ever forgive me?"

Carter placed her hand on Kambree's shoulder. "I really don't know, but I wish she would. I guess only Kendra can answer that."

The bedroom door opened. It was Kambree's mother. "Anyone want to go shopping down the street?"

"Sure, Miss Phyllis!" said Carter.

Kambee's mother chuckled. "I thought you might be interested. See you both at the car in five minutes."

The two girls scrambled to prepare for their shopping trip. Moments later, they could be heard laughing and giggling as they rushed out the door. Carter now clearly understood the benefits of forgiveness.

Ask Yourself...

1. In our story, how did Carter benefit by forgiving Kambree?

2. Kendra chose not to forgive Kambree. How was this hurtful to Kendra?

3. Can you identify someone you need to forgive? Explain.

Last Word

In our story, Kambree made two big mistakes. First, she promised Carter and Kendra tickets to a concert, only to later realize that she had no tickets for the girls. And to make matters worse, Kambree chose not to inform them of the bad news as they waited by the phone. This angered both Carter and Kendra, although we know they chose to deal with their anger in completely different ways.

Kendra chose not to forgive Kambree. Due to this, Kendra held a grudge and continued to feel angry day after day. Kendra felt miserable each time she saw Kambree at school as it reminded her of the concert she had missed. Did Kendra gain anything by not forgiving?

Carter handled her anger differently. She chose to forgive. Once Carter's mother convinced her daughter to show forgiveness, Carter's anger quickly disappeared and was replaced with a peaceful feeling. Carter soon realized that choosing to forgive makes it much easier to be a happy person. It also made it possible to remain friends with Kambree.

In our story, Carter's mother explains that she always keeps in mind that God chooses to forgive her on a daily basis. When we understand that we regularly need forgiveness from God, we should also understand that God expects us to show forgiveness, too, just like Him.

Remember, none of us are perfect. We all need forgiveness in our lives, including you. So step up and show others a forgiving heart. You'll feel better, the person on the receiving end of your forgiveness may feel better, and most importantly, you will please God. If you have not practiced forgiveness on a regular basis, start today. You will not regret it.

Chapter Five

UNDERSTANDING DISCIPLINE

Verse: No discipline seems pleasant at the time, but painful. Later on, however, it produces a harvest of righteousness and peace for those who have been trained by it.

Hebrews 12:11

Do You Believe In Ghosts?

"How much farther is it to the haunted house? We've been walking down this trail for over an hour," Hayes complained.

Aaron laughed because it hadn't been nearly that long. "We'll be there soon. Anyway, haven't you always wanted to see a ghost?"

Hayes smiled. "Come on, Aaron. You and I both know that there's really no such thing as ghosts."

"You'll feel much differently about ghosts in just a few minutes," Aaron confidently stated. "Speed up or get left behind." After a pause, he added, "Believe me, you don't want to get left behind out here."

The two boys continued to follow the winding trail through the forest. Hayes noticed that the deeper they ventured, the thicker the growth was around them. This made everything appear much darker, giving Hayes a creepy feeling. He did not share this with his friend, believing Aaron would only make fun of him.

Neither boy spoke as they continued down the path. Occasionally, Hayes looked back over his shoulder, believing he'd heard rustling in the brush or a twig snap just out of his line of sight. Hayes shivered. *It's just my imagination getting the best of me. There's nothing out here to be scared of.*

At that moment Aaron stopped.

He turned to Hayes and whispered, "Be very quiet and follow me."

Aaron led Hayes off the trail they'd been following. They crept through a maze of trees and high weeds until they came upon two old, rusted barrels. Aaron crouched behind the barrels and motioned for Hayes to do the same.

Hayes obeyed without hesitation. "What are these barrels doing here?"

"I found them one day when I was exploring," Aaron said, his voice still low. "Take a look."

Slowly, Hayes rose up and peered over the barrels. To his surprise, he could see the roof of the haunted house directly in front of him, but trees and brush made the rest of it impossible to view from where they were hiding.

Hayes's heart began to race. "Is that the haunted house?" His voice shook.

"It sure is," Aaron replied, grinning. "Are you ready to wake up the ghosts?"

"What do you mean 'wake up the ghosts'?" Hayes didn't like the sound of that.

Aaron reached into one of the barrels with both hands and came out with two large rocks.

"What are those for?"

Aaron tossed one over. "Every time I hide here, I throw a rock towards the house. It must anger the ghosts, because sometimes they start moaning."

Hayes shook his head in disbelief. "Do you really expect

me to believe that?"

"There's only one way for you to find out. On the count of three. One, two, three!"

The two boys hurled their rocks toward the haunted house and quickly ducked behind the barrels. A second later glass shattered in the distance.

"You broke a window!" exclaimed Aaron gleefully.

"Maybe it was your rock that broke it."

Aaron began laughing so hard that he could barely speak. "Man, I was just joking with you! I don't really believe in ghosts, and that house isn't haunted. I can't believe I tricked you into breaking that window."

Hayes's face burned. He grew angrier and angrier as Aaron ridiculed him.

Suddenly an eerie moan pierced the air. "Wooo! Woooo!"

The smile vanished from Aaron's face, replaced by fear. "What was that?"

"How would I know?" Hayes snapped. "It sounded like a ghost."

"I've been out here a million times and have *never* heard anything like that!" Aaron exclaimed.

"It sounded like it came from behind us," Hayes said. "Not from the haunted house."

The two boys turned towards the moaning noise. Hayes detected movement in some bushes just a short distance away. He gulped. Suddenly, two figures appeared from the brush.

Instead of being terrified, both Aaron and Hayes were able to breathe a sigh of relief. One of the figures was Aaron's older brother, Barry.

"What's the big idea, Barry?" Aaron cried. "What're you doing out here?"

Barry began laughing. "You should've seen the look on your faces. We had you both scared to death!"

"Very funny," replied Aaron as the two older boys

continued laughing.

Barry continued, "I think the real question is what are you two doing out here?"

Aaron gave them an innocent smile. "Nothing really. You know that I like to look for deer tracks. I was showing Hayes where the deer like to cross the trail."

"So what're you doing off the trail?" Barry asked as he folded his arms.

Aaron was at a loss for words. "We, uh, just came over here to, uh, rest for a minute."

Barry motioned to his friend who had yet to speak. "Logan here might be interested in why you just broke a window in his dad's hunting camp."

Hayes broke his silence. "I'm sorry Logan. I didn't know it was your dad's camp. I thought it was a haunted house."

"A haunted house?" Logan shook his head. "What gave you that crazy idea?"

Everyone looked at Aaron, who could only stare at the ground with embarrassment.

Logan sighed. "All I can say is that my dad is going to be really mad when he finds out what you two did."

Aaron's eyes widened. "You're not really gonna tell your dad, are you?"

"*Of course* he's telling his dad," said Barry. "Somebody's gotta pay for the window."

"Come on, guys," Aaron pleaded. "Can't we work something out?"

Logan rolled his eyes. "Let's go, Barry."

Barry glared at the younger boys as he turned to leave.

It seemed like a long journey back to Aaron's house as Hayes considered what type of discipline he might receive once his parents learned that he had broken the window.

The next day at school during recess

"I can't believe it's still raining," Aaron griped. "So much for finishing our soccer game."

Hayes nodded. "I know. Recess is always *so* boring when we can't go outside."

"Hey guys!" yelled a voice from behind. "What's going on?"

"Oh, hi, Jeff," replied Hayes as he turned to greet his friend.

"I heard you two got into *a lot* of trouble yesterday," Jeff said. "Did you really break those windows?"

"It was only one window," Hayes quickly pointed out.

"So what did your parents do to you?"

Hayes spoke first. "I won't get an allowance until the window is paid for. Also, I don't get to play video games for a month. Worst of all, I can't visit any friends for the next two months."

"Man, your dad is mean," said Jeff. "I've never been punished that much in my entire life."

"I wouldn't really say that my dad is mean. Isn't that what parents are supposed to do when we break rules?"

"Are you kidding?" asked Jeff. "I've *never* been grounded like that."

Jeff turned to Aaron. "You've been awfully quiet. What did your parents do to you?"

"They didn't really say much about it."

"You didn't even lose your allowance?" questioned Hayes.

Aaron shrugged. "Nah, my dad just paid for the broken window and never really mentioned it to me. He never punishes me."

Jeff smiled. "That's good, because you'd always be grounded!"

The three boys all joined in laughter.

"You sure are lucky to have parents that let you do what

you want," said Hayes.

"Yeah," added Jeff. "You're the luckiest kid in the school."

Phone call ten years later

"Hello, son," said Hayes's dad.

"Hey, Dad. What's going on?"

"Not much. I just came in from sweeping the driveway. So how's college life?"

"Oh, good for the most part. This week I've got a lot of studying to do. Final tests are coming up."

His dad laughed. "I'm sure you'll make it all right. It's hard for me to believe that you'll soon graduate from college. Where has the time gone? It seems like only yesterday that I was teaching you how to ride a bicycle."

"I know. Just think, in a few weeks, I'll not only be finished with college, I'll be looking for a job."

"You'll be fine. You're very well prepared."

Hayes grinned. "Yeah, Dad, thanks to you."

"What do you mean?"

"Well, you always did a good job of teaching me right from wrong and how to accomplish things. You made sure there were always consequences when I did something bad." Hayes laughed. "I can also remember getting really mad at you when I got into trouble."

Dad joined in the laughter. "Yeah, I recall you believing that you were the unluckiest kid in the world when I grounded you, while some of your friends never seemed to receive any form of discipline."

"Speaking of my past friends, I guess you heard about Aaron?"

"Yes, son, I did."

"I hate to hear that he's in jail again. I was hoping that he'd learned his lesson after the first time."

"Me, too. He's made a lot of bad decisions."

"I remember that he was one of the kids in school that I thought was so lucky. Back then, he could do *anything*, and his parents never said a word. Of course, now I can see that maybe he wasn't so lucky."

"Well, I hope you know that I didn't enjoy grounding or restricting you. I did it because I wanted to teach you to live a life that would be pleasing to God. The Bible has many verses that encourage parents to properly discipline their children. Your mom and I have done our best in raising you and your sisters in the way that the Bible teaches."

Hayes nodded. "Dad, when I was younger, I never dreamed I would say this, but thanks for taking the time to discipline me and lead me in the right direction."

"You're welcome."

"By the way, I was calling to remind you that I won't be coming home this weekend. I think I'm gonna need extra time to study for my final exams."

"Perfectly understandable. We'll look forward to seeing you when you do come."

"All right, Dad. I'll talk with you soon."

"I love you."

"Love you, too."

Ask Yourself...

1. What is discipline?

2. True or False: Discipline is one of many ways for a parent to show love for their children.

3. Can you name three people that provide discipline in your life? List them.

Last Word

In our story, discipline is referring to the actions taken by parents to train their children to live life in a manner pleasing to God. Discipline requires providing children with rules and consequences. Consequences occur when rules are not obeyed.

There are many forms of discipline used by parents. Discipline may include spanking, taking away privileges, or giving a child additional chores. Whatever form of discipline is chosen by your parents, it is intended to be unpleasant in order to persuade you to follow rules and improve your ability to make good choices in the future. So think about it this way: Parents are preparing you to live in a manner that is pleasing to God. This makes discipline one of many ways a parent can show love for you...although it sure does not seem like it at the time!

For many of us, discipline is received most often from our parents. Still, there are others that you may receive discipline from. An example would be your teachers. They have many rules that must be followed. Without the ability for them to discipline, many students would not follow *any* rules. Imagine what school would be like without rules or any form of discipline? It would surely be disastrous for both students and teachers.

Our verse states that discipline is "painful" at the time it is administered. Always try to keep in mind that these "painful" experiences assist you greatly in becoming a successful person. When you receive discipline, it's extremely important for you to understand the need for it in your life. Understanding discipline makes it easier for you to accept, which will result in greater benefit to you. Yes, it's designed to be an unpleasant experience, but believe it or not, it's unpleasant for *all* involved, including your parents!

Remember, the best way to avoid discipline is to follow rules and make good choices. This can make life much more pleasant for you because you are living each day in a manner pleasing to your parents and even more importantly, to God.

Chapter Six

NOT JUDGING BY APPEARANCE

Verse: But the Lord said to Samuel, "Do not consider his appearance or his height, for I have rejected him. The Lord does not look at the things man looks at. Man looks at the outward appearance, but the Lord looks at the heart.

I Samuel 16:7

Mirror, Mirror, On the Wall

Outside the church classroom

"Jenna, you look great!" squealed Brooklyn as she raced up to her friend. "Where did you get that skirt?" She laughed. "I am *so* jealous."

Jenna smiled as she struck a pose. "I thought I might need to bring out my best today. After all, I have to persuade the judges to choose me as the 2012 Bible Rally Representative."

Kady snickered as she joined the conversation. "Are you kidding? When the teachers see you, there's no doubt who they'll want to represent our church." Kady lowered her tone. "Where's your competition?"

"Ashley? I saw her downstairs a few minutes ago," Jenna whispered. "She looked scared, like she'd just seen a ghost. On second thought, maybe she looked that way because she wasn't wearing any makeup."

51

The three girls broke into a chorus of giggles.

After catching her breath, Jenna said, "She doesn't really seem that prepared. Surely I don't have anything to worry about."

"Of course you don't," Brooklyn said. "The judges will love you. You look amazing, not to mention you're a great speaker. Think of how many pep rally speeches you've given. On the other hand, Ashley is shy. I'm not even sure if she knows how to talk. How can she possibly represent our church….especially in the weird clothes that she chooses to wear!"

Once again, the three girls joined in laughter at Ashley's expense.

Kady looked down at her watch. "Oh, Jenna, you'd better hurry! It's about time to get started."

Jenna quickly hugged her friends and rushed inside to meet the judges.

Inside the classroom

All that could be heard was the clop-clop of Jenna's heels as she marched towards a couple of folding chairs directly in front of the judge's table. Jenna carefully studied each judge as she took her seat. She smiled as she sat down, purposefully making eye contact with each, hoping to make a good impression. Jenna's confidence increased as she recognized each judge. She was able to recall positive experiences with the majority of them.

This could be easier than I thought.

The head judge, Miss Judy, spoke first. "Welcome, Jenna. We'll get started just as soon as Ashley arrives."

At that moment, the door creaked open. Ashley slid through and meekly approached the group.

Once again, Miss Judy was the first to greet the new arrival. "Good morning, Ashley. Have a seat next to Jenna.

It's time for us to get started."

Ashley seemed unable to speak. Head lowered, she nodded and awkwardly found her place.

Miss Judy smiled at them. "All right girls. Over the past weeks, I've discussed the qualifications and duties of a Bible Rally Representative, in particular what our church is looking for. As you know, we started with quite a few candidates. Now here, on the final day, we're down to the two of you. You should both feel very proud." Miss Judy paused for a few seconds as the girls received applause from the group of judges. Once the applause subsided, she continued. "As you both know, the final part of the selection process is for you to explain why you should represent our church. We flipped a coin to determine who is to speak first. Jenna, you're up."

Jenna stood and confidently stepped up to the judge's table. "Ladies and gentleman, I want to thank you for giving me the opportunity to speak with you today. There are many reasons that I should be the 2012 Bible Rally Representative. For two years, I've worked very hard at school to represent others, so I have a lot of experience. This year, I'm serving as captain of the pep squad, and I also won Miss Crab Queen second runner up just a few weeks ago. I'm sure you all heard about that. But that's not all. I'm a hard worker. Once a month, I volunteer to sing at the nursing home. Since they love my singing, I don't mind the work too much. *And believe me*, I will definitely go shopping before the rally and promise that none of you will be disappointed with my wardrobe. I will represent you all in style! Well, that's about it... and once again, I want to thank you all for giving me this opportunity."

Jenna turned to go back to her seat. Before taking a step, she quickly swung back around to face the judges. "Oh, I forgot one thing. I haven't missed a church service in almost three months."

"Thank you, Jenna," replied Miss Judy.

Everyone's attention then turned to Ashley.

"You're welcome to speak now," Miss Judy said softly.

Despite Miss Judy's mild mannered invitation, Ashley appeared startled. She sprung from her chair, realizing her moment had arrived. In contrast to Jenna stepping forward to address the judges, Ashley moved to the side of her chair and a few steps back. She took a deep breath.

"Good morning," she said shyly. "Thanks for considering me. It's an honor to be in the final two, especially since so many kids wanted to represent our church."

Jenna smiled to herself as she detected a nervous quiver in Ashley's voice.

"My goal is to do my very best to let everyone know about special things in our church, but mainly our mission programs. I talked with church leaders and found out some interesting information. Ten years ago, our church offered no opportunities for our members to go on mission trips to other countries and tell them about God. At that time, our church had no missionaries. In the last ten years, our church has offered many mission trips. We started with just Mexico and now people in our church also have the chance to go to China, Nicaragua, Ukraine and the Czech Republic. And guess what...now there are nine missionaries that used to be members of our church. If picked as a representative, I plan for my project to show how mission trips grow missionaries."

To Jenna's dismay, she could no longer detect any nervousness in Ashley. She appeared to grow more confident with each word she spoke.

"And one last thing," Ashley said, "I have a video presentation prepared on last summer's trip to Mexico. I believe it shows how an ordinary kid like me can be used by God to do good things for Him in another country. Maybe it will help other kids see that they can do it too. That's all."

Ashley retreated to her chair. She no longer slumped, but now sat upright, appearing to study each judge in the same manner Jenna had earlier. She watched as the judges passed small slips of paper to the center of the table. Miss Judy closely examined each and returned her attention to the two girls.

"Once again, I want to say that both of you should be proud. I believe that I speak for each judge when I say that either of you would make a great representative…but as you know, we can only choose one representative. Miss Judy paused for a moment, which seemed to add to the suspense. Finally, she spoke. "Without any further delay, I would like to announce that the 2012 Bible Rally Representative is… Ashley!"

Jenna sat in stunned silence as Ashley jumped from her chair. "I can't believe it! Thank you, thank you!" Ashley cried as she hugged Jenna. Ashley was so excited that she didn't notice that Jenna didn't return her embrace. Miss Judy chuckled as she watched Ashley.

"I've got to call my dad!" Ashley resembled a windmill as she clumsily scuttled out of the room. Miss Judy looked down at Jenna. She realized that Jenna was upset and felt she might need a little encouragement. But before Miss Judy was able to speak, Jenna lashed out. "How could you all pick her over me? Ashley looked like an absolute wreck, while I took the time to look my best. Do you seriously want someone like her to represent you?"

Miss Judy's smile vanished. "I expected much better from you. First of all, there's nothing wrong with Ashley's appearance. Second, this was not a beauty contest. If someone led you to believe that it was about appearance, they were sadly mistaken."

Jenna was now staring down at the floor, refusing to make eye contact. Miss Judy continued, although in a softer tone. "Jenna, I want to read you a verse I came across the other day."

Miss Judy reached behind her and brought up an old,

worn Bible. She set it on the table and began thumbing through its pages. Jenna did not look up as Miss Judy searched for the verse. "Here it is, **I Samuel 16:7**. '**But the Lord said to Samuel, "Do not consider his appearance or his height, for I have rejected him. The Lord does not look at the things man looks at. Man looks at the outward appearance, but the Lord looks at the heart."**"

Miss Judy looked up. "Jenna, when our panel of judges deliberated over who our representative would be, appearance was not considered. As this verse teaches, we should focus more on a person's heart and less on how a person looks."

Jenna continued to hang her head, now in shame. A quiver could be detected in *her* voice as she whispered, "I'm so sorry." Jenna rose from her chair. Without looking up, she quickly turned to the door. Embarrassed, she could not leave the room fast enough.

Ask Yourself...

1. Pretend that you were one of the judges in our story. Would you have chosen Jenna or Ashley as a representative? Explain.

2. Our story's scripture says "Man looks at outward appearance but the Lord looks at the heart." What does that mean?

3. Think about your friends at school. Do they remind you more of Ashley or Jenna? Explain.

Last Word

Our story's verse is about "appearance" and "heart." Appearance simply refers to the way we look. "Heart" refers to the type of person we are based on our thoughts, beliefs, and actions. While many people may focus on how others look, God is looking at our heart. This shows us that we should focus more on having a good heart and less on trying to please others with our appearance.

In our story, Jenna was surprised that she wasn't chosen to represent the church. Jenna believed that she should have won based on the way she looked and the nice clothes that she wore. Ashley won because she placed the focus on God and her church, not herself. Jenna gave little indication that she was focused on God. How about you? Do you put God first? We should all take time to study our behaviors. We need to figure out if we are more like Ashley or Jenna. Chances are that we sometimes resemble Jenna, putting our own self-interests over God. By placing God first, you'll have a happier and more content heart. Give it a try starting today.

Chapter Seven

OBEYING YOUR PARENTS

Verse: Children, obey your parents in the Lord, for this is right. "Honor your father and mother"—which is the first commandment with a promise—"that it may go well with you and that you may enjoy long life on the earth."

Ephesians 6:1-3

Play Ball!

"Hey, dad, it'll be kind of weird not having a sling on my arm at school today," Cade said from the backseat of the car.

Cade's father smiled as he turned down the radio. "Well, Dr. Washispack instructed you to wear the sling for three weeks, and three weeks ended yesterday."

"I know it was only for a few weeks, but it felt like I had worn it *forever*."

His father laughed. "Yeah, I know. When we're doing things that we like, time passes quickly. On the other hand, time seems to pass very slowly when we're involved in something we don't particularly enjoy."

Cade shifted his attention to the city baseball complex. "*That's* where I need to be." He pointed towards the ball fields. "I can't wait to play baseball again."

Cade's father braked as they approached a traffic light.

"Cade, I know you love baseball, but you've got to be patient. Hopefully your doctor's appointment after school will shed some light on how well your arm has progressed."

Cade crossed his arms over his chest. "Are they going to let me start throwing again?"

"We'll see, but don't be surprised if he tells you to take it easy for awhile."

"But Dad, practice starts in two weeks!"

His dad nodded. "I realize that, but you can't rush the healing process."

"I know, I know. Please don't remind me again."

They reached the school parking lot. "Now remember, no throwing at recess or *any* activity that could aggravate your injury."

"Okay, Dad." Cade grabbed his backpack and exited the car, managing a half-hearted "good-bye" as he closed the door.

After school at Dr. Washispack's office

Cade was tired of waiting. "Mom, what's taking so long? The doctor left our room a long time ago."

Cade's mother gently placed her arm around her son's neck. It was always easy for her to tell when he was worried. "The doctor will be back soon. He has to study the x-ray to be sure you didn't chip a bone in your arm. He believes the problem is a stretched ligament."

Cade didn't immediately reply. He appeared to be in deep thought.

"Uh, w-what did the doctor say a ligament was?"

"It's the flexible, stretchy tissue that connects your bones together."

A light tapping at the door halted their conversation. Dr. Washispack entered the room and sat on a nearby stool. Smiling, he wheeled himself over to Cade. Just like Cade's mother, the doctor could read the troubled expression on his face.

He patted Cade on the knee as he began to speak. "As you know, I decided to x-ray your arm today. It showed no bone damage. Based on today's examination *and* the fact that you've reported no pain over the past few weeks, I'm confident that your ligament was not torn, only stretched."

Dr. Washispack attempted to continue, but Cade could not contain himself. He felt as though he were about to burst. "Woo-hoo! Did you hear that mom? My arm's all right. I can play baseball!"

The doctor stopped him. "You'll be able to play, but you'll probably need to limit your throwing for a while."

Cade did not welcome this news. He slumped down in his chair and stared at the floor. Dr. Washispack took note of this and tried to encourage his patient. "When we tested your arm earlier, we found it to be much more flexible than the arms of most kids. This actually helps you to throw a baseball as hard as you do. Unfortunately, it also may have attributed to your injury. I have decided to refer you to a physical therapist."

"What can we expect from physical therapy?" Cade's mother asked.

"It will put Cade through various exercises that will allow his arm to strengthen. They will also teach some exercises for Cade to do at home."

Cade looked up at the doctor. "How long will I have to go to physical therapy?"

"It's hard to say. You'll be asked to go for as long as the therapy benefits you. It usually takes around a month with this type of injury, but I would hate to say for sure. They may even teach you a safer throwing motion, which could take a little longer."

Cade gasped. "*Longer?* Baseball season starts in just a few weeks!"

Dr. Washispack grinned at Cade in a reassuring manner. "If you work really hard and do exactly what the physical therapist tells you to do, I bet you'll have a great baseball season."

This seemed to lift Cade's spirits a bit. "All right, I'll do my best."

Dr. Washispack patted Cade on the back and offered him an assortment of candy. The meeting seemed to end on a positive note.

Two weeks later

Cade slowly trudged over to the same wooden bench he'd become accustomed to sitting each recess for the past two weeks. His parents had given him strict orders not to take part in any activities at recess until his physical therapist gave him a clean bill of health. Cade sat down and opened his math book. He yawned as he considered the past two weeks. *At least I haven't had any homework since I finish it every day at recess.* Cade looked up from his math book and watched his fellow students on the playground. He quickly spotted his friends and could tell they were forming teams for a football game. Disappointed, he shook his head and tried to concentrate on his math assignment. Before long, Cade had lost all awareness of the activity surrounding him as he worked. He quickly completed two of the three pages of his homework.

"What's up, Cade?" shouted a familiar voice.

Startled, Cade almost dropped his math book. He laughed as his friend, Bruce, approached. "What're *you* doing here? I figured that you'd be busy playing football."

"That's what I'm here for," Bruce said. "The older boys have challenged us, and we need you *right now*. Come on."

Cade couldn't hide his frustration. "You know I can't play. I've got to rest my arm. What're you trying to do, get me in trouble?"

"Of course not. You can still rest your arm. We don't

need you to throw at all, just catch."

"My parents made it very clear that I can't play until the doctor says it's okay. Do you want me to be grounded for the rest of my life?"

Bruce laughed. "I doubt that playing one game of football can get you into *that much* trouble. This is the first time that the older boys have actually agreed to play against us. This is our one big chance to beat them."

Cade's mind was racing. *What do I do?* He knew that his parents would be completely against this, but would it really be so bad to play just this once? After all, his friends didn't even need him to throw the ball, just catch it. Cade pondered over his dilemma a moment more and came to a decision. Grinning at Bruce, he leaped from the bench. "What're we waiting for? Let's show those older guys who rules!" The two boys strategized as they dashed off to join the game.

The contest lived up to Cade's expectations. Despite the older boys having an edge in size and strength, Cade and his buddies were able to match their opponents score for score. Cade felt great, being on the receiving end of two touchdown passes. Also, Bruce had made good on his promise. Cade had not been asked to throw the ball even one time.

The boys quickly gathered in a huddle. "All right guys, if we can stop them for a couple more plays, the game ends in a tie," Bruce whispered.

Shorty laughed. "Yeah, they'll never live it down."

Bruce nodded. "Same play as last time."

The older boys quickly snapped the ball. Their quarterback stepped back and heaved the ball into the end zone. To Cade's delight, the ball landed harmlessly beyond their opponents' outstretched arms.

"We still have one more play!" shouted one of the older boys. "If we don't get to run our last play before the bell rings, the game doesn't count."

Hearing this, Bruce became frantic. The younger team

was *so* close to showing everyone that they could play just as well as the older boys. He searched for the football. Finally, he spotted it. It had bounced far beyond the ball field. "Cade, go get the ball!" Bruce screamed. "You're closest to it!"

Cade quickly spotted it. He made a mad dash towards it, feeling the same sense of urgency as Bruce. He reached the ball in no time. Grabbing it up, he raced back towards the ball field. His teammates were all jumping up and down, waving their arms, urging him to toss it back to the older boys for one last play.

"Hey, Bruce. Catch!" Cade threw the ball with all of his might. He heard a *pop!* Sharp pain shot through his arm. Though he instantly realized his mistake, it was too late. He jogged back for the final play. Even watching Shorty bat down the older boy's pass didn't lift his spirits. Cade slowly walked away, clutching his arm as his teammates celebrated. They didn't even notice his absence.

Why didn't I listen to my parents? My arm is killing me, and my baseball season is over.

As Cade entered the school office to report his injury, his tears had nothing to do with the pain in his arm. He'd disobeyed his parents, and now he had to tell them what he'd done.

Ask Yourself...

1. Why is it your parent's responsibility to set rules and guidelines for you to follow?

2. At this time, how well do you obey and honor your parents? Explain.

3. Our story ended with Cade phoning his parents with news of his injury. How do you imagine that type of conversation with your parents would make you feel? Explain.

Last Word

Our story's scripture focuses on expectations that God has for children and their parents. The key words in our story's verse are "obey" and "honor." Obeying your parents is to follow their direction. Honoring your parents is to show them love and respect.

"Obey your parents" is a simple command, yet often difficult for young people to follow. Throughout the ages, they've questioned their parents' ability to set rules and guidelines for them. It's not uncommon for kids to believe that they are fully capable of "running their own lives." So often, young people make decisions based on what brings immediate pleasure, while parents make decisions for their children based on teaching the difference between right and wrong and helping them develop into responsible adults. Parents are better equipped to make these decisions. They've had years of instruction from their own parents and have also learned from years of life experiences.

Our scripture makes it clear that it's in God's design for children to obey and honor their parents. Scripture does not state that young people must agree with their parents, just show obedience and honor. To disobey one's parents is to directly disobey God. By following God's command in our scripture, you are not only showing your parents proper respect, you're giving God obedience and honor.

Chapter Eight

BEING UNSELFISH

Verse: Now a man came up to Jesus and asked, "Teacher, what good thing must I do to get eternal life?"

"Why do you ask me about what is good?" Jesus replied. "There is only one who is good. If you want to enter life, obey the commandments."

"Which ones?" the man inquired.

Jesus replied, "Do not murder, do not commit adultery, do not steal, do not give false testimony, honor your father and mother and **love your neighbor as yourself**."

Matthew 19:16-19

A Stranger in My House

Mrs. Foshee stared out of the kitchen window, focusing on nothing in particular. She could've been a statue; she hadn't moved for minutes. Suddenly, her stove's timer sounded, breaking the silence. She quickly removed some chocolate chip cookies from the oven and glanced at her watch. *Porchia will be home soon.* She began to get anxious. *I've got to quit worrying about her vocabulary test. After all, making a C on her report card wouldn't be the end of the world.* Still, that was all she could focus on.

For the next hour, Mrs. Foshee kept herself busy with chores around the house. She started by sweeping the back porch and then watered her rose bushes. Just as she finished, she heard a sound coming from the garage and hurried to the door. Mrs. Foshee knew she was overreacting a bit, but she was dying to know her daughter's test score. As she reached for the door, Porchia burst into the room, clearly happy about something.

"I hope that big smile means what I think it does."

Instead of answering, Porchia showed her a paper that she was hiding behind her back.

Her mother's eye widened. "Ninety-five! Are you serious? I'm so proud of you!" She gave her daughter a big hug. They began brainstorming ways to celebrate Porchia's accomplishment.

One hour later

"By the way, Porchia. What vocabulary word did you miss?"

"I missed the word *selfless*. I misunderstood and wrote the definition of the word *selfish*."

Her mother nodded. "That's understandable. Unfortunately, most of us hear the word self-ish much more than self-less. Do you know what it means to be selfless?"

Porchia thought for a moment. "We learned that it means, uh, showing unselfish concern for the well-being of others."

Her mother smiled. "Very good. It's important that you always remember that God expects us to be selfless, caring as much about the needs of others as much as we care about ourselves."

"I know, Mom. I won't forget."

One month later

Porchia looked over the school cafeteria, searching for a familiar face. As she scanned the large room, she saw students of all ages. Many were talking in groups while others appeared to be busy trying to complete unfinished homework assignments. Porchia looked down at her watch. She still had fifty minutes before her first class.

"Porchia, over here!"

Porchia recognized the voice. Smiling, she turned to see her best friend, Brandi, who quickly led her to a table near the back of the cafeteria. Once there, Porchia could see a couple of her classmates huddled together, chatting away.

"Look who's here," Brandi said as the pair approached the table.

Becky and Scottie looked up from a magazine that they were sharing.

Becky smiled. "Why are *you* here so early?"

Porchia sat down. "My dad had a business meeting."

"Hey, Porchia," said Scottie. "I heard some big news about you and your family." He gave her a mischievious grin.

Brandi glared at him. "You are so rude! If Porchia hasn't brought up the adoption—" She stopped in midsentence, eyes wide, realizing what she'd let slip. Brandi was relieved to see that Porchia was still smiling.

Porchia chuckled. "Guys, don't worry about it. I'd planned on giving you the news today."

"Good," said Scottie. "I heard that your family is getting a girl who is our age, not a baby. Is that true?"

Brandi rolled her eyes at Scottie, clearly wishing he'd hush.

Porchia took a deep breath. "Here's what I know. The girl that my parents are adopting is twelve years old and has been living at an orphanage in a country called Nicaragua. Her name is Ana."

"Does she speak English?" asked Brandi.

"Not much. Everyone in Nicaragua speaks Spanish. Ana will have to learn English once she arrives. Mom and Dad are flying to Nicaragua in three weeks to get her."

"This is *so* cool!" Brandi exclaimed. "You've always said that you wanted a sister." Brandi glanced at Becky, who hadn't said a word. "You've been awfully quiet. Don't you think it's neat?"

Becky shrugged her shoulders. "I guess so." She looked the other way.

Porchia was puzzled. Typically, Becky was very talkative and the center of attention. "What's wrong? Aren't you happy for me?"

Becky looked up. "Will you be mad at me if I tell you exactly what I think, even if it's not what you want to hear?"

Porchia's smile faded. "Sure. I want to know what you think."

Becky shrugged. "Okay then. Do you really want another person in your home? Just think. *All* of the attention will be on her. Your parents will be busy buying *her* stuff and helping *her* learn how we do things in this country. Believe me. That will be a full-time job. How will they have anything left for you?"

Brandi gasped. "I can't believe you just said that."

Porchia turned to her. "It's all right. Don't be mad at Becky. I wanted to know what she thought about the adoption, and she told me."

"But she's wrong!"

"It doesn't matter. That's how she feels." *And she may have a point.*

"Let's change the subject," said Scottie. "What do you guys plan to get me for my birthday?" Even though there was a new topic of discussion, Porchia couldn't stop thinking about what Becky had said.

After school

"Where's dad?" asked Porchia as she plopped into her father's recliner.

Her mother entered the living room and sat down with a

stack of folders. "He had a meeting at the church tonight."

Porchia showed no reaction. Instead, she picked up the remote control and began flipping through the television channels.

"I've got some good news," her mother said.

That got Porchia's attention. She set down the remote control. "I could use some good news. What is it?"

Smiling, Porchia's mother handed her one of the folders. She hastily opened it and studied the contents. "Airline tickets? Are these for our summer vacation?"

"No, honey. Read the ticket."

Porchia examined the tickets closely. Her excitement died, and she closed the folder.

"Tickets to Nicaragua," her mother said. "The church has decided to help us with the costs so you'll get to be there when we meet Ana! Isn't that wonderful?"

"Wonderful," Porchia echoed, her voice flat.

Her mother was caught off guard by her reaction. "I can tell that something's bothering you. Why aren't you excited?"

Porchia stared at the floor and didn't speak.

"Spill it," her mother coaxed. "It's time to tell me what's wrong."

Porchia knew her mother would demand an explanation for her behavior. She quickly rehearsed in her mind what to say. "Uh, a lot of kids at school have been talking about Ana and the adoption. Some of them believe that Ana will need so much from you and Dad that I will get totally left out. They say that I won't get any attention, and that I won't get to go shopping as much. They even said that I won't get as much for my birthday because of Ana." Porchia rocked back and forth in her chair, her eyes glued to the carpet.

Her mother sighed. "Do you remember the word that you missed on your vocabulary test?"

"Sure," snapped Porchia. "It was *selfless*, which really

has nothing to do with any of this."

"Do you remember what *selfless* means?"

"Selfless is showing unselfish concern for the well-being of others."

Her mom nodded. "Exactly. Does selfless describe *your* attitude right now?"

Porchia thought for a moment. Suddenly feeling guilty, she whispered, "No, ma'am."

Her mother took a seat next to her. "Your dad and I have prayed a lot about this, and we believe that adopting Ana is what God is asking our family to do. It may mean less shopping trips and fewer gifts for *all of us*. Dad and I learned long ago that there are much more important things in life besides what money can buy us. We believe that Ana needs us as *we need her*. She'll be one of the greatest gifts that we could ever hope to receive."

Porchia had never felt more ashamed. "I'm sorry." She hugged her mother. "I was being selfish. I promise that I really do want Ana as a sister. From now on, I'll think about others as much as myself."

Porchia's mother smiled. "That's great, honey. What you just said reminded me of something I read in the Bible last week."

"What's that?"

"Love your neighbor as yourself."

Porchia grinned, "That means to be selfless, *not* selfish!"

Her mother laughed. "I think you've got it!"

For the remainder of the evening, Porchia enjoyed time with her mother, making a list of "selfless acts" that they could do for Ana once she joins the family.

Ask Yourself...

1. Our story's verse says "Love your neighbor." Is God strictly referring to people that live in your neighborhood? Explain.

2. What has God specifically asked us to do when He commanded, "Love your neighbor as yourself."

3. Can you identify an opportunity to show selflessness? Think of a person in need and show them you care by performing a selfless act.

Last Word

"Loving your neighbor as yourself" is very difficult for many people. The world that we live in seems to reinforce selfish behavior and influence us to care about our own "wants" more than the actual "needs" of others. God wants us to care for our neighbors as we care for ourselves. To do this, we must show concern for others and help those in need.

When Jesus said, "Love your neighbor as yourself," he was not simply speaking of people that live in your neighborhood. He was referring to anyone that you come in contact with. Consider the amount of people that you see each day. That is *a lot* of opportunities to "love your neighbor as yourself."

In our story, Porchia decided that the needs of Ana were as important as her own. She chose not to show selfishness, although she was temporarily influenced by a friend to think only of herself. By resisting this temptation, she was able to enjoy the prospects of a new sister and also please God.

It's very important to avoid selfishness. There are few better ways to show love for your neighbor than through performing selfless acts. The key is to focus on giving instead of receiving. You'll find that this will actually *give you* a great feeling inside!

Chapter Nine

MAKING FRIENDS

Verse: My dear brothers, take note of this. Everyone should be quick to listen, slow to speak and slow to become angry.

James 1:19

Who's The New Guy?

"It's time, August!" shouted his mother as she stared at her watch. "You don't want to be late for your first day at your new school."

"Yeah, I'd really hate for that to happen." August laughed sarcastically as he loped into the kitchen. "What're we waiting for? Let's go."

His mother sighed as her son slung his backpack over his shoulder as he passed, missing her nose by inches. She shook her head in frustration. "Please be careful."

August showed little reaction as he continued into the garage.

He's nervous about attending a new school, August's mother thought. *He always acts like this when he's hiding his true feelings.* She followed her son through the garage and onto the sidewalk.

"We're headed in the right direction, right Mom?"

"Yes. Your school is barely a block away. I'm sure it

won't be long before you become familiar with the whole neighborhood. It seems like a—."

August cut in angrily before his mother could finish her thought. "We know it's impossible for me to know the neighborhood. I don't even know where everything is in my own house! How long have we been here, *two whole days*?"

It was obvious to August's mother that her son was very upset about moving to a new town. This did not surprise her. After all, he'd just left the only home he'd ever known. "You know that we had to move quickly. Your dad's new job required him to be available for work right away."

"I know, I know. Dad just *had* to take this job and make me leave all of my friends behind. Tell him thanks a lot."

August's mother chose her words carefully, hoping to calm her son. "Moving here has been a big change for all of us. I'm sure that as long as you just be yourself, you'll have no trouble making new friends. I bet in no time that you'll enjoy your new school."

The school came into view. August quickened his pace. His stomach seemed to tighten more with each step. "See ya," he muttered as he quickly turned away from his mother and began jogging down the sidewalk.

"Try to have a good day!" she called as August dashed off. *Not a good start*.

Lunch Time

August grabbed his lunch tray as he completed the cafeteria line. He turned to what seemed like an endless row of tables with students scurrying in all directions. He searched with uncertainty for a vacant chair, finally spotting an empty table near the back of the noisy cafeteria. *That looks good*. August moved in the direction of the table. *Maybe I won't get any more ugly looks from these kids. Hopefully, I won't even be noticed*.

76

August felt as though he were part of a maze as he dodged and darted through the cafeteria traffic. Finally, he reached the table and sat down.

"Hey, can we sit with you?"

Startled, August whirled around to see three boys that he recognized from his Geography class. He didn't know what to say. "Uh, sure, uh, sit down."

The three boys sat across the table. August's heart was racing. He felt as though it might pound right through his chest. *Is this some sort of joke or do these guys really want to meet me? Maybe I can impress them so they'll like me. This could be my only chance to make friends.*

The boy who first spoke smiled broadly. "I'm Dalton and this is Jaren and Mason." He pointed to the other boys.

"My name is August. I just moved here from Louisiana."

Mason grinned. "I heard Louisiana has lots of alligators!"

Although August had never seen a live alligator before, except at the zoo, he felt as though he must develop an exciting story. "Oh, yeah. I fought alligators all of the time. My brother, Todd, and I would run them out of our yard with baseball bats."

"You mean you weren't scared?" Jaren asked, wide eyed.

"Nah, it's no big deal if you do it every day."

Jaren looked over at Mason.

"Hey Mason. Do you remember the time when those dogs got into your dad's trash and we had to—"

August cut in, hoping to regain the spotlight. "Did I mention that one of those alligators was more than ten feet long?"

Jaren didn't seem to appreciate the interruption. "That's long," he mumbled.

"I've always heard that crocodiles get a lot bigger than alligators," commented Dalton.

"Well, the person that told you that didn't know what they were talking about!" August quickly snapped back.

"Louisiana grows the biggest gators in the world, even bigger than *any* crocodile."

The three boys looked at each other, taken aback by August's defensive manner. No one spoke. August became uncomfortable with the awkward silence. He noticed that the palms of his hands were beginning to sweat. He nervously looked down at his lunch tray, searching for something to say. He decided to start a new topic. "Hey guys, what's the food like around here? Not this school food, but around town. Any cool places to eat and hangout?"

"Oh, yeah," Mason said. "Everyone around here loves Matty Ice. They have burgers and pizza, but everyone really goes for their ice cream and games. My favorite is—"

"I doubt anything's better than the shrimp and crab I've eaten in Louisiana," August interjected. "Sometimes Todd and I caught our own and my dad cooked them that very night. I already miss it."

Dalton appeared to have lost interest after another interruption. "It sounds like you're really missing your home," he responded halfheartedly.

"You're right about that. I left only two days ago and it feels like it's been forever. I miss my home, my friends, my neighborhood, my school, *and* the food."

Jaren regarded August sympathetically. "I remember being the new kid here three years ago. Everything seemed so different from what I was used to, and having—"

August butted in. "I can tell that this place will *never* replace my home and I really don't see myself ever liking it. I'm sure there isn't anything here that's as good as in my hometown. *And nothing is going to change my mind.*"

Jaren sat quietly with his arms crossed, feeling slighted after yet another interruption from August.

Mason had enough. "I'm, uh, not trying to be mean or anything, but you're not very much fun to talk to. Every time someone tries to say something, you cut in. It seems like you talk and talk, but never listen."

August felt his cheeks burn. He was now so mad that he couldn't even think straight. Without realizing it, he began yelling. "If you don't like what I have to say, you can all go sit somewhere else. I didn't ask for any of you to sit with me anyway!"

Mason looked at his friends. "Come on, guys. Let's go."

Dalton glared at August. "Yeah, we don't need any of this."

"You got that right," added Jaren. "Let's get out of here."

"That's the smartest thing you've said all day!" All alone now, August realized that he was shaking. Before long, his anger was replaced with sadness and disappointment. *I knew they didn't care about being my friend. They came over here just to pick on the new kid.* August had lost his appetite. He slowly rose and returned his tray. Head lowered, he left the cafeteria.

At home after school

August sat slumped on his beanbag chair, thumbing through a family photo album. He focused on a set of photographs taken at last year's Summer Festival in Louisiana. One particular photograph caught his attention. It was taken of August and his two best friends just as they had gotten off a roller coaster that the older boys had thought they were too scared to ride. He smiled to himself, remembering how much fun he had with his friends that night.

"What are you looking at?" asked his dad from the bedroom doorway.

August looked at him in surprise. "What're you doing here? I thought you'd be at work."

August's father smiled as he sat down on the floor next to his son. "I wanted to see how your first day of school was. I know that changing schools can be difficult at first."

Although he was tempted to again share his dismay over moving, he decided to simply answer his father's questions. "It didn't go so well. None of the kids like me."

August's dad asked his son to recount the day's events. His father listened closely as August described it. Though Dad quickly realized what had gone wrong, he allowed August to completely finish sharing before saying a word. He looked thoughtfully at his son. "August, I think you have the opportunity to make a few adjustments in your attitude and behaviors. If you do, you'll have little trouble enjoying your new school."

"Are you saying that everything was *my* fault?"

"I'm not blaming anyone for your bad day, but I think I can give you a few tips that will help you to make new friends and feel better about your new school."

"Like what?"

His father chuckled as he attempted to lighten the mood. "Glad you asked. First, you have to just be yourself. Don't feel like you have to stretch the truth or try to impress others. Remember, you made a lot of friends in Louisiana without that."

"What else do I need to do?"

"Well, I know it's fun to talk and let others know more about *you*, but it's even *more* important to listen. Being a good listener allows others to know that you care about them and their ideas. A good listener is usually great at making friends."

August felt bad about the way he'd acted at school. "I guess I didn't do a whole lot of listening today."

His dad patted him on the back. "That's all right, August. There's always tomorrow."

"Is there anything else I need to do differently?"

"I can think of one more thing that I believe will really help. You seemed to quickly anger when things didn't go your way today. When a person is slow to anger and remains calm, they typically go through life a happier person, and those around them are usually happier too!"

"I really messed up a lot today, didn't I?"

"It's okay. We all make mistakes, and it was just *one* day. You have many days ahead to make corrections. And remember, God will be there with you. Say a quick prayer if your day is headed in the wrong direction.

"Can we pray right now?" asked August.

"Sure thing, August. Now I can tell you're on the right track!"

Ask Yourself...

1. August annoys others when he chooses to constantly talk and show no interest in listening to others. Why is listening so important?

2. The story demonstrates that it's important to remain in control of one's emotions when angry. August was quick to anger when feeling nervous and uptight. What makes it difficult for you to control your anger?

3. Is it wrong to experience feelings of anger? Explain.

Last Word

In our story, August has difficulty making friends with others because he talks and talks, showing no interest in listening. August is not the only person that has made this mistake before. Many people believe that being a good talker is the most effective skill necessary to make friends. While communicating your thoughts is important, being a good listener can be *more* important. Listening, not talking, is the best way to demonstrate that you care about someone. It shows that their thoughts and feelings are important to you. Showing that you care is a necessary part of any friendship. Being a "good listener" makes that easy.

Another problem August encountered was his inability to control his temper. This ruined an opportunity for him to make new friends. We all become angry from time to time. The key is to remain calm. Avoid raising your voice, using words that are hurtful, and *definitely avoid fighting!* A great way to control anger is to get away from what has caused you to feel it. This gives you time to calm down and think more clearly.

Another tip in controlling anger is to have an understanding of what type of things seem to make you mad. Sometimes, being aware of what angers you will help you to avoid situations that will most likely get you riled up.

Remember our story's verse. Be quick to listen, and slow to speak and become angry. By keeping this in mind, it will greatly assist you in building healthy friendships throughout your life.

Chapter Ten

TURNING DISCOURAGEMENT INTO OPPORTUNITY

Verse: Now I want you to know, brothers, that what has happened to me [put in prison for spreading God's word] has really served to advance the gospel. As a result, it has become clear throughout the whole palace guard and to everyone else that I am in chains for Christ. Because of my chains, most of the brothers in the Lord have been encouraged to speak the word of God more courageously and fearlessly.

Philippians 1:12-14

If Only I Were Perfect

Cassie climbed into the backseat, joining her little sister, Allison Grace. Tonight lacked the usual family chatter as her father pulled out of the gymnasium parking lot and headed home. Allison Grace squirmed uncomfortably as she eyed her sister, waiting for her to speak. Cassie sat still, head lowered and eyes closed. Allison Grace then turned her attention to the front seat where her mother and father sat. They stared straight ahead and didn't seem to want to talk, either. Finally, Allison Grace decided that she'd be the one to break the silence. She turned to her big sister. "Cassie, just think. If you had made that last shot, your team would've won the championship."

Allison's mother quickly turned to the backseat. "Allison Grace, that wasn't really a great choice of words. It would've been much more supportive to simply tell your sister that she played a good game."

Allison Grace frowned. "I was just telling the truth."

Cassie broke *her* silence. "Don't you think that I already know that I lost the game? I don't need you or anyone else reminding me."

Cassie's father intervened before the conversation became more heated than it already was. "Now that's enough. Let's all calm down and look at the facts." He cleared his throat before continuing. "Cassie, you have absolutely nothing to feel bad about. You are one of the best players on the team, and you're only in the tenth grade. I think you even led your team in scoring tonight. We're all very proud of you."

"But I let the team down when they needed me most." Before her father could reply, Cassie added in a much stronger tone, "I should just quit!"

Her dad remained calm. "I believe you may be saying things out of anger that you really don't mean, so we'll just drop this conversation for now. We'll discuss it another time when you feel more like talking."

"I really doubt it'll be anytime soon."

Cassie's father turned his attention to Allison Grace. "No more talk about the basketball game, all right?"

"Yes, Dad."

The remainder of the ride home was quiet and uneventful.

When they arrived, Allison Grace jumped from the vehicle and dashed over to her mother. She whispered, "Is Cassie really quitting the team?"

Her mother quickly changed the topic as she led Allison Grace into the house.

A few days later

Cassie's father could tell that his daughter was still upset over the basketball game. Anytime the subject was approached, Cassie was adamant that she'd "let everyone down" and that she "should quit the team." Her father believed that her disappointment would soon pass, and she'd be looking forward to the next season. Still, he decided to talk with her, hoping to improve her perspective on the situation. Since Allison Grace and her mother were out grocery shopping, Cassie's dad felt the time was right to speak with her. He entered the living room where she sat. "What's going on?"

"Nothing much," murmured Cassie as she studied over her History homework. She didn't bother looking up.

Her father sighed as he took a seat on the couch next to her. "I think it's time that we have a serious talk about the ball game and how it's affecting you."

Cassie rolled her eyes and looked up at her father. "Do we really have to? That's the last thing I want to talk about."

"You're not handling the loss very well, and you need to consider how your behavior is affecting Allison Grace."

"Allison Grace? What does *she* have to do with this?"

"I understand that you've felt discouraged ever since the game ended, but you need to accept that things may not always go your way in basketball or anything else you do in life. I mean, even the professional players aren't perfect. They miss shots too."

"That's what my coach and some of my friends have been trying to tell me."

"Well, it's natural to feel emotions such as disappointment when you come up a little short, but it's something that *everyone* experiences."

Cassie lowered her head. "I know you're right about this. Maybe I've just been feeling sorry for myself."

Cassie and her father sat quietly for a few seconds before something occurred to her. "I still have no idea what this has to do with Allison Grace."

Her father smiled. "You need to understand that Allison Grace really looks up to you. She tries to be *exactly* like her big sister. If she's been watching you lately, what kind of message do you think she's getting?"

Cassie was taken aback and had no immediate response.

"What I really want you to think about is how often she's heard you mention quitting the team. Personally, I don't think you'd do it. I *think* that you just let frustration get the best of you."

"You're right. I love basketball and would never quit."

"But does Allison Grace know that?"

"No, I suppose not," Cassie sheepishly replied.

"If your sister constantly hears you talk about quitting when things aren't going your way, how do you think she'll act in the future when she becomes discouraged?"

"She'll think it's okay to be a quitter. And I don't want her to be like that."

"You have a chance to turn this into something positive."

"How's that?"

"You can talk with Allison Grace about the negative things you've said."

Cassie nodded. "Yeah, I need to explain to her that I never truly wanted to quit the team and that quitting is usually the wrong thing to do. From now on, I'll handle my disappointment better."

Her father was relieved. "That's good to hear you say. And if you can teach your little sister a valuable lesson in all of this, you can be proud that you've taken a difficult situation and turned it into an opportunity to help her."

Cassie smiled. "I'll have a good talk with her as soon as she gets home."

Ask Yourself...

1. Why is it important to show good behavior even when you feel disappointed or discouraged?

2. Identify a circumstance that you exhibited poor behavior when things did not go your way. What can you do differently next time?

3. Consider all of the people you know. Who would you want your behavior to be most like? Explain.

Last Word

In our lifetimes, we will experience a great variety of emotions. Happiness and joy are two that we hope occur frequently. Unfortunately, it's impossible to avoid experiencing negative emotions such as discouragement and disappointment from time to time. We do not live in a world that allows everything to work out favorable for us. Although it can be challenging, reacting in a positive manner during difficult times is a great way to show others that God is a major part of your life. In our story's verse, Paul did not show discouragement even though he was placed in prison for telling others about Jesus. This was noticed by many and it encouraged them to share God's word with more determination.

In our story, Cassie handled discouragement poorly by feeling sorry for herself and saying that she should quit the basketball team. Her inability to deal with discouragement set a bad example for her little sister. We must always keep in mind that others are watching us and that our behaviors may influence people in a positive *or* negative way. Try to set a good example for them. Remember, it's our responsibility as Christians to do so. Hopefully, Cassie learned a lesson and next time will be able to teach Allison Grace (or maybe even a friend or classmate) simply through her actions.

The next time that you feel discouraged or frustrated, react in a manner that will please God. It's an ideal time to demonstrate to others that you have God in your life.

Chapter Eleven

AVOIDING THE USE OF HURTFUL WORDS

Verse: I am in the midst of lions. I lie among ravenous beasts – men whose teeth are spears and arrows, whose tongues are sharp swords.

Psalm 57:4

The Invitation

Josh once again found himself in an all too familiar position. He could no longer count the number of times that he'd sat on the same old worn out sofa, waiting to meet with the school principal. He shifted uncomfortably as he eyed the door to the principal's office, anticipating another unpleasant meeting. He knew that Mr. Nugent would not be happy to see that he was in trouble for the second time in three days.

He looked over at the school secretary. "Miss Mary Ann, do you think it'll be much longer?"

"It's hard to say, Josh. Mr. Nugent is in a meeting right now."

Josh looked around. He found nothing of interest as he scanned the room. Becoming bored, he began thinking about why he'd been sent to see the principal. *It's not even my fault that I'm here. If Kylan hadn't smarted off, I wouldn't have pushed him.* At that moment, a lady entered the office. Josh groaned as he recognized Mrs. Howard, the mother of a classmate that he didn't like. Jealousy stabbed at him. *Tim acts like he's the smartest kid in school and thinks he's great because he won the golf tournament last week. I can't stand him.*

Mrs. Howard didn't notice Josh as she approached the secretary.

Miss Mary Ann looked up. "Good afternoon. It's nice to see you. Are you here for Tim?"

"Yes. I've got to get him to the doctor before three o'clock. His allergies have been such a problem this spring."

"How is Tim getting along with his little sister these days?"

Mrs. Howard smiled. "He's doing better than we could have *ever* expected. For example, the other day, Jackie asked me to join her for a tea party with all of her dolls, but I didn't have time. She began crying and guess who came to the rescue?"

"Tim?"

Mrs. Howard laughed. "That's right. Although he hates the thought of playing with dolls, he hated seeing his little sister upset even more."

"It sounds as though Jackie has a wonderful big brother."

Although it went unnoticed, Josh was now smiling broadly as he watched Mrs. Howard leave the office.

The next morning

Students milled around their lockers, either chatting or gathering their belongings in preparation for their first class. Josh was among them, talking with friends about his visit to the principal's office.

Josh laughed. "Mr. Nugent told me that I would no

longer be given detention hall because he doesn't believe it will change my behavior."

"So what happens the *next* time you're in trouble?" his friend Ray asked.

Josh smiled slyly and did not give an immediate reply in order to heighten his friend's curiosity.

"Tell us," said Bucky.

"He said that he would suspend me for a *whole* week!"

"Are you serious?" asked Bucky. "My older brother told me that no one has been suspended from this school in years."

"That's right," replied Josh with a nod.

Ray looked puzzled as he studied Josh. "Why are you smiling and acting like you've done something good? I wouldn't be smiling if *I* were the one getting into trouble all of the time."

Josh glared at Ray and was about to confront him when something else caught his eye. Looking down the hallway, he saw Tim heading his direction. Josh had been hoping to meet up with him. Now he would get his chance. "Watch this," Josh said as Tim approached. "Hey, Tim, have you been to any good tea parties lately?" Josh looked back at his friends and winked.

Tim was caught off guard. "What're you talking about?"

"Your mother was in the school office yesterday bragging about you playing tea party with your little sister. I heard it straight from her, so we all know it's true."

Tim was clearly shocked that Josh knew this and wasn't sure how to respond.

"Look at him!" exclaimed Josh as he pointed at Tim. "You can tell he did it. He's not even trying to deny it."

Josh's friends began laughing and chimed in with their own hurtful remarks at Tim's expense.

Tim's stomach tightened and he began to feel sick as he struggled for something to say. "I-I don't like tea parties or playing with dolls. I was just trying to cheer up my little sister."

"That's so sweet." Everyone began to laugh even harder.

By now Tim's heart raced, and he was beginning to sweat. He knew it was a no-win situation. They'd laugh at him no matter what he said. Abruptly, he turned and dashed down the hallway, far enough to escape Josh and his friends. When he realized that they hadn't followed, he found a quiet place where he could have a moment to himself. He was almost in tears.

After school

Josh sat in his bedroom playing video games. He decided to take a break and raid his Grandmother Edith's cookie jar. Tossing his game aside, Josh noticed that something had slipped out of his backpack—an envelope. He picked it up and quickly ripped it open. To his surprise, it was an invitation to a birthday party. Excited, he read the message on it. All of a sudden, his mood changed. He set the invitation aside and slumped to the floor. Sadness and guilt replaced his excitement. The invitation was from Tim.

"How could Tim have invited *me* to his birthday party after the way I treated him?" Josh said aloud. "After humiliating him in front of everyone, I don't deserve an invitation." Josh sat quietly and assessed his behavior. *The only reason I acted like that is because I'm jealous that Tim makes better grades, and he beat me in last week's golf tournament.*

Josh's appetite was gone. It was now *his* turn to feel bad as he regretted his actions towards Tim. For the next hour, Josh curled up on the floor and considered what he needed to do to make up for his poor behavior. He realized that it was time to make some serious changes in his life.

Ask Yourself...

1. Our story's scripture states "tongues are sharp swords." What does this mean?

2. If you hear someone speaking words that may be hurtful, is it acceptable to repeat these words to others even if you know the information is true?

3. How should you react if someone has spread hurtful words about you?

Last Word

The story's scripture focuses on how damaging our words can be when we speak poorly of others. Psalms 57:4 compares hurtful words to being in the "midst of lions" and "among ravenous beasts." The verse further compares hurtful words to weapons such as spears, arrows, and swords. Comparing words to weapons of war illustrates the harmful effects of gossip and name calling. The scripture clearly shows that God frowns on this type of behavior. Unfortunately, talking badly about others is fairly common in everyday life. Situations arise almost every day in which one may choose to gossip or unjustly criticize others. Try to avoid this type of behavior. Even if we hear negative statements that happen to be true, it's best for the words not to be repeated. Seldom does any good come from this.

We must consider that there could come a day when *we* are the subject of gossip or unjust criticism from others. Maybe you already know how it feels for bad things to be said about you. When hurt by words, it may be tempting to respond strongly with damaging words of your own. Remember, as tempting as it may be, it's best not to copy the bad behavior of others. Quickly go to God in prayer and allow him to lead you through these difficult moments.

In our story, Josh uttered many hurtful words and encouraged others to join in. Later, he felt terrible about what he'd done. He realized that his actions were not because Tim was a bad person. They were strictly due to jealousy. Hurtful words are often spoken when one is not truly happy or satisfied with their own life. This is important to remember when we are on the receiving end of hurtful words. Pray that the speaker of these words will make positive changes to lessen their desire to hurt others. Tim forgave Josh and even invited him to a birthday party. This motivated Josh to make changes. Had Tim responded back to Josh with hurtful words, Josh's behavior would have only gotten worse. Tim's behavior is an example of what God would like to see in us all.

Chapter Twelve

BEING PATIENT

Verse: A patient man has great understanding, but a quick-tempered man displays folly.

Proverbs 14:29

Are We There Yet?

Matt and Mallory raced through the Science and History Museum in an attempt to be the first in line for the popular Australia Exhibit. Mallory skillfully picked her way through the crowd, leaving the speedier Matt far behind. She smiled to herself as she found a place in line with only a few kids in front of her. Seconds later, Matt arrived huffing and puffing, attempting to catch his breath. Instead of taking his place at the back of the line, he stepped directly in front of Mallory. This angered her. "Hey, what's the big idea?"

Matt looked back over his shoulder. "It was *my* idea to see this exhibit. You wouldn't even know about it if it weren't for me."

"I wish Mr. Holloway wouldn't have paired us together. I'd rather be with one of my friends."

Matt smirked. "You're not the only one."

"You'll be sorry. I'm going to tell Cheryl about your behavior."

The smirk on Matt's face turned to a glare. "Cheryl doesn't

scare me one single bit. And just because Mr. Holloway says that she's in charge of us today doesn't make her my boss." Matt searched the crowd. "Where is she, anyway?"

Mallory knew all too well why Cheryl was not present. She was beginning to regret that they had slipped off the first time Cheryl looked the other way. At that very moment, Cheryl approached.

"*There* you two are." Cheryl placed her hands on her hips. "May I remind you that field trip rules require each pair of children to have a high school chaperon. And more importantly, if your chaperon reports *any* bad behavior to your teacher, you'll spend the day sitting on the school bus."

"First of all, I'm not a child. And what's a chaperon?" Matt asked, pretending not to know.

"*It's the person in charge of you!*" To Matt, Cheryl sounded like she really meant it. "Well anyway, I'm here to inform you that Mr. Holloway's class is meeting at the museum café. It's time for lunch."

Matt crossed his arms in defiance. "Are you kidding me? Look how close we are to seeing the Australia Exhibit. We can't go now."

Cheryl looked down at Matt. "It's time for lunch and that's an order from your teacher."

Matt glared at her. "That's not fair! I'm not about to lose my place in line!"

Somehow Cheryl remained calm. "Cool it, Matt. You don't want to get into trouble. Anyway, Australia's not going anywhere. You'll get to see the exhibit right after you eat."

"Everybody thinks they can boss me around," Matt mumbled as he left his place in line and angrily stomped away.

Mallory and Cheryl followed him into the café.

Inside the cafe

Chatter filled the air. Kids could be heard laughing and

sharing museum experiences. All appeared to be having a great time as they enjoyed hot dogs and hamburgers. Despite Cheryl's persuasive efforts, Matt refused to eat lunch or interact with classmates. He sat alone at a corner table, still fuming over being told to vacate his place in line. He focused solely on a clock that hung directly overhead, waiting for lunch to end.

As the lunch break wound down, Matt corralled Cheryl and Mallory, urging them to hurry back to the line. In order to avoid a tantrum, Cheryl took them back to the Australia Exhibit. To Matt's disgust, the line was now much longer.

"Look how long the line is *now*." Matt groaned as he once again stepped in front of Mallory.

"Just be patient, Matt," replied Cheryl. "I'm sure it will move fast."

"Are you going to the exhibit with us?" Mallory asked Cheryl.

"No, but I'll be watching you from over there." Cheryl motioned towards some nearby benches.

As Mallory watched Cheryl walk away, she decided to make peace with Matt. "I hear that the Australia Exhibit will have a real train take us over a bridge that has a pond of crocodiles under it."

"I know," Matt replied without even turning to face Mallory. "I'm ready to see *live* animals. I'm tired of looking at dinosaur bones."

"Adyson told me earlier that we'll get to feed the kangaroos by hand."

Matt turned to Mallory. "Don't believe everything you hear."

Suddenly the Australia Exhibit loudspeaker announced, "We are having mechanical problems with our train. We apologize for any inconvenience that may result from this delay. The problem should be corrected soon."

Matt threw his arms up in the air in frustration. "I knew

we should have stayed in line instead of going to lunch! Now we probably won't get to see it!"

Mallory chose her words carefully. She did not want Matt to take his anger out on her. "They said our wait won't be long, so there's no need to worry. We'll be on the train soon."

Matt didn't reply or even acknowledge that Mallory had spoken. He became unusually quiet. Ten minutes passed without a word. Finally, he turned to Mallory. She was shocked to see that he was smiling. "Mallory, this delay is getting longer and longer...and look at how many kids are in front of us in this line. What do you say we cut in front of the younger ones?"

"That's mean. How would *you* feel if someone did that to you?"

Matt ignored the question. "I figured you'd be too scared to do it." He glanced over at Cheryl. She appeared to be busy texting. "Come on. Cheryl's not even watching us."

"No way. I'm waiting in line just like we're supposed to."

"Well, you had your chance." Matt edged away, smiling. "See ya."

Mallory shook her head as she watched Matt advance towards the front of the line. Sure enough, he secured a spot in front of the smaller children that he had targeted. It did not appear to Mallory that he received any type of resistance. Matt was now in better spirits and no longer worried about the time of day since he would be the next to board the train. Suddenly, he felt a tap on his shoulder. Believing that one of the younger students was confronting him, he jerked around. Only it was not a child. "Mr. Holloway!"

"You look surprised to see me," Mr. Holloway said.

Matt was now nervous. "Wh-what can I do for you, sir?"

"You can come with me." Mr. Holloway gestured to Cheryl, standing behind him. "Cheryl has filled me in on your behavior today."

"What're you talking about?" Matt pretended as if he didn't know.

Cheryl answered him. "For starters, you ran away from me this morning. Then you threw a temper tantrum before lunch. And to top things off, you just cut in front of all of these kids."

Mr. Holloway shook his head. "Matt, this is unacceptable behavior. Come with me right now."

"But I'll miss the exhibit. Please don't make me go."

Mr. Holloway looked at Cheryl. "Please join Mallory in line while I walk Matt to the bus."

Matt cried, "I don't want to leave! Give me another chance!"

Mr. Holloway ignored Matt's pleas as he led him out of the museum. Just as they exited the museum, a voice boomed over the loud speaker. "The mechanical problems we earlier experienced have now been corrected. Please move forward to board the train at this time."

Mallory moved forward just as the loud speaker had requested. She realized that her patience had paid off as she stepped onto the platform to board the train.

Ask Yourself...

1. Matt and Mallory spent the day together at the museum. In what ways were their behaviors different?

2. Is it easier for a patient person to stay out of trouble? Explain.

3. Identify times that you need to be more patient. How will showing patience benefit you?

Last Word

Patience is the ability to wait on something in a calm, controlled manner. A patient person does not complain or lose control of his or her behavior while waiting. This typically results in having less difficulty getting along with others and staying out of trouble. Our scripture tells us that individuals who lack patience are often "quick-tempered" and "display folly." Folly means to act foolish.

In our story, Mallory remained patient despite enduring delays as she waited to enter the Australia Exhibit. Her patience was rewarded with an enjoyable tour of the exhibit. Matt was a different story. He was extremely impatient. Unlike Mallory, he was quick-tempered and anxious. The inability to control his behavior resulted in breaking rules and ultimately having to suffer the consequences. Due to his lack of patience, he spent most of the day feeling angry and miserable.

Although not enjoyable, it's a fact of life that we must spend much of our time waiting. Seldom does a day go by that we don't have to wait for something. This can really test our patience. Since we are forced to wait so often, patience can really come in handy. It allows us to remain calm and think clearly. Showing patience each day will make those around you happier...*and you'll feel better, too*. Patience helps you to make good choices and more easily exhibit behaviors that are pleasing to all. Don't *wait* any longer. Work on being a more patient person starting today!

Chapter Thirteen

DEALING WITH PEER PRESSURE

Verse: Do not follow the crowd in doing wrong. When you give testimony in a lawsuit, do not pervert justice by siding with the crowd and do not show favoritism to a poor man in his lawsuit.

Exodus: 23: 2-3

Curtain Call

"I love Friday afternoons," said Candice as she watched her classmates run up and down the gymnasium floor. She looked on as they engaged in a variety of games, ranging from basketball to shuffleboard.

Eva glanced at Candice. "I like Fridays too, mainly because I'd rather end the school day hanging out in the bleachers instead of doing schoolwork."

Candice nodded. "It's like an extra recess."

At that moment, Lindsay joined Candice and Eva. She had just completed a taxing game of chase with some boys from her class. She sat down and wiped sweat from her forehead.

Eva rolled her eyes, not impressed. "Lindsay, I don't see why you like running around with those boys. It seems to me that they spend more time teasing you than actually chasing you."

Lindsay laughed at Eva's comment. "They only tease me because they're mad they can't catch me."

"Well, it doesn't look like much fun to me."

Smiling, Candice turned to Eva. "*To me*, it looks like Lindsay is having more fun than we are. All we've done is sit here in the bleachers watching everyone else."

Eva placed a hand on each hip and countered, "Are you saying that you'd rather play with those boys than talk to me?"

Candice decided it would be best not to reply in order to keep peace. Eva was known for her fiery temper and the last thing Candice wanted was to get her riled up. Many moments passed before someone spoke.

"Did you know that a long time ago this school had plays and music shows up there?" Eva asked as she motioned towards the stage just beyond the concession stand.

"Where did you hear that?" asked Lindsay.

"My sister, Julie, told me about it."

"I've always wondered what it looks like back there," said Candice. "Everything is hidden by those old curtains that hang in front of it."

Lindsay agreed with a nod. "Maybe one day they'll open them and let us have a peak."

Eva had a gleam in her eyes. "Hey, I've got an idea. See the door to the left of the stage that says 'Do Not Enter'? When the teachers aren't looking, what do you say we go back there and check things out? Everything's so loud and crazy in here, there's no way they'll even notice that we're gone."

Clearly excited, Candice voiced approval of Eva's idea. "That sounds cool! It'll be our own little adventure. The boys in our class will be *so* jealous that they didn't come up with the idea. Count me in."

Eva and Candice turned their attention to Lindsay. They could tell by her expression that she didn't share in their excitement. "Lindsay, what's the matter. You don't like my idea?"

Lindsay began to feel butterflies in her stomach. She knew that it was against the rules to go behind the stage, yet she didn't want her friends to be upset with her, either. She cleared her throat as she searched for a response. "Uh, didn't Mr. Cangelosi say that if he ever catches anyone back there, they'd get suspended for three days? I think it's against the rules because a first grader broke his ankle snooping around back there."

This angered Eva. "Do you mean to tell me that you'd rather run around with those boys than to do something exciting with us? It makes me wonder if we're really best friends."

Candice sided with Eva. "It seems like you never want to do anything that *we* want to do. You only think of yourself."

Before Lindsay could defend herself, Eva looked over at Candice and conversed as if Lindsay were not present. "I think I know what Lindsay's *real* problem is—she's scared."

Candice nodded. "I think you're right. She's not really acting her age, much younger."

Lindsay began feeling terrible and started to second guess herself. *Great. What have I done now? My two best friends are mad at me again. Maybe I'm overreacting and going behind the stage really isn't a big deal. And maybe they're right and I'm just being a baby.* Lindsay forced a weak smile. "Okay, guys, I'll go."

"Good girl, Lindsay," Eva said. "I knew you wouldn't let me down!"

Lindsay didn't reply. As they headed towards the stage door, she wondered why she always seemed to give in to Eva and Candice.

With all of the activity on the gym floor, it was not difficult for the girls to get by the teachers unnoticed as they slipped behind the stage door. They were pleased that it wasn't completely dark. Sunlight filtered through some stained windows, which assisted the girls in maneuvering around the room. As they surveyed the area, they came upon discarded tables, broken desks, and a multitude of storage boxes. Nothing was of great interest to them.

Eva sneezed. "This place is disgusting. There's so much dust in here, I doubt anyone's cleaned in years."

Something sparked Lindsay's interest. "Hey, Candice. Is that a door to your left?"

Candice peered into the dimly lit area. "I think it may be. Let me check." Candice clumsily waded through piles of rubble that blocked what appeared to be a door hidden just behind a large bookshelf. As she neared the bookshelf, her question was answered.

"Come on, guys. It *is* a door. Maybe it'll lead to something."

Eva and Lindsay carefully followed Candice's path up to join her. Once there, Eva grasped the doorknob. "Ready?"

"Now remember," Lindsay said. "We've got to get back to the others soon."

This irritated Eva. "I know, I know. Just drop it, okay?" Eva glared as she opened the door. It was completely dark inside.

Candice felt along the walls for a light switch. "Here it is." She flipped it on and the room went from complete darkness to full illumination. The girls winced as they entered the room, attempting to adjust to the light. They closed the door behind them. "Look at all this cool stuff!"

"I've never seen so many costumes in my life," said Lindsay. "All of this must've come from the school plays they had here."

"Of course it is." Eva began rummaging through what appeared to be a box of dresses.

The girls completely lost track of time as they investigated *every* storage box and clothing rack in the room. They laughed and joked as they tried on costume after costume, pretending to be characters from books and movies that they were familiar with. Eva, dressed like a rock star, studied herself in a mirror. Lindsay, dressed as a medieval warrior, wielded a plastic sword in all directions. Candice, now in a vampire outfit, crouched behind a crate, pretending to hide from her next unsuspecting victim.

Suddenly, the door burst open and Principal Norsworthy entered the room. All three girls screamed as his booming voice yanked them back from their fantasy worlds. "What are you three doing back here? We've been looking everywhere for you." He cleared his throat. "Sorry I scared you, but we've all been worried sick for over an hour. Your absence has caused quite an uproar."

Lindsay was visibly shaken. "P-Principal Norsworthy, we didn't m-mean to worry anyone. I, uh, guess we just didn't realize how much time had passed."

"Girls, school's been out for more than twenty minutes, the buses have left, and your parents have been notified."

"My parents!" Eva dropped her head. "I'm gonna be in *so* much trouble."

"You're right about that. The three of you have broken a serious school rule. Please follow me. We need to call your parents and let them know that you're all right."

Lindsay left the room feeling awful, regretting that she'd allowed Eva and Candice to pressure her into doing what she knew was wrong. It seemed like a long walk to the school office, knowing what lied ahead. *Why did I let them do this to me again? I could've stayed out of trouble if I'd just thought for myself instead of letting them think for me.*

Ask Yourself...

1. What is peer pressure?

2. In our story, what do you believe was Lindsay's biggest mistake?

3. Do you believe that Eva and Candice acted like "true friends" towards Lindsay? Explain.

Last Word

Peer pressure occurs when friends or acquaintances pressure you to think and act in a manner that *they* desire. This is usually done by making you feel as though you will not be accepted as a friend *unless* you act or think in the same manner that they choose for you.

In our story, Eva and Candice use peer pressure in order to persuade Lindsay to break a school rule. They were successful in controlling Lindsay's behavior by making hurtful remarks and questioning whether she was truly their friend. That was the moment Lindsay needed to realize that if Eva and Candice were *truly* her friends, they would've accepted her decision not to go behind the stage. Does this ever happen to you? Think about it.

The story's scripture warns us about peer pressure. It says "do not follow the crowd in doing wrong" and gives some examples. God gave you a mind that is fully capable of making your own decisions. Refrain from choices that are made to simply please those around you. When faced with these difficult moments, pray to God for the wisdom and strength to resist peer pressure. In the long run, you'll be glad you did.

Chapter Fourteen

BEING HONEST

Verse: The Lord detests differing weights and **dishonest** scales do not please Him.

Proverbs 20: 23

Show Me The Money!

John had worked hard over the weekend selling tickets to his school's annual fundraising event. He was glad that the money raised would assist the school in purchasing new computers and lab equipment, but his main motivation to raise money was to win the competition held between all of the classes. This year, it was announced that the class who sold the most spaghetti dinner tickets would be rewarded with an all-day fishing trip at the lake and a pizza party. Since the deadline to turn in money had arrived, winning the fundraiser was the hot topic of conversation. He couldn't wait to get updates from his friends concerning ticket sales.

As John entered the classroom, he immediately spotted his friend, Bart. He rushed over to him. "Hey, how many tickets did you sell over the weekend?"

Bart smiled. "I sold twelve more. How about you?"

"Lucky for me, *everyone* was at my house Saturday night for my sister's birthday party, so I really racked up—*twenty more!*"

"That's great since we were only six dollars ahead of Miss Michele's class last Friday."

John nodded. "I know. Hopefully, the rest of our class did their part and sold a lot of tickets, too."

"Well, they plan to announce the winner at the end of the day."

At that moment, Kyle and Bryan peeked into the classroom. They were students from Miss Michele's class.

"Hey guys. You'd better hope that your class sold *a lot* of spaghetti tickets this weekend because our class sure did!" Bryan grinned. "Tara just told me that she sold *fifty* more tickets. It looks like *my* class is going to the lake."

"Who are you kidding?" Bart responded. "*No one* can sell that many tickets in one weekend. Believe me, when the money's counted at the end of the day, Miss Paulette's class will be declared the winner."

Kyle laughed. "Whatever you say. Not trying to change the subject, but if you want some *real* competition, meet us in the weight room at recess. I'll bet Bryan and I will beat you at that, too."

All of the boys chuckled as they parted ways. John didn't mention the ticket sales again, but he couldn't help but worry after hearing that Tara had sold fifty tickets. He wondered, *Was that even possible? Surely she couldn't sell that many tickets in just one weekend. Bryan's probably up to one of his little tricks.* As class started, he struggled to pay attention to his school work.

In the weight room

For a while, the boys forgot all about the fundraising competition and focused strictly on weightlifting. They enjoyed competing against each other, seeing who was best at each exercise. At the sound of the bell, Bryan and Kyle quickly gathered up their belongings.

112

"Kyle and I don't have much time," Bryan said as he lifted his gym bag. "Our class is at the other end of the building, and we can't be late. You know what happens when you're late for Mr. Norton's class."

John smiled. "I'd run if I were you."

Bryan and Kyle took his advice and dashed down the hall. As they departed, something slipped out of Kyle's pocket. John and Bart hurried over to see what it was.

"Look at that," said Bart. "Kyle lost his money."

John picked up the roll of bills and began to count. "Hmm, twelve dollars, and there's a check too."

"The check is for thirty-six dollars," commented Bart. Then something more caught his eye. "Hey, it says here on the check that it's for tickets to the spaghetti dinner."

"*More* money for Miss Michele's class," John groaned. "It looks like we may lose the contest on the very last day."

There was a long pause before either boy spoke. Finally, John broke the silence. "Bart, tell me what you think about this. What do you say we return the twelve dollars to lost and found and act like we never saw the check?"

Bart didn't understand. "Why would we want to do that?"

"Isn't it obvious? When Kyle realizes that he's lost his money, the first place he'll go to find it is the lost and found. After all, I do want Kyle to get his money back. He's my friend."

Bart was even more confused. "But why don't you also return the check?"

John rolled his eyes. "Don't you want to win the pizza party and the field trip? We'll deny *ever* seeing the check. If Kyle gives this check to Miss Michele, they'll have *even more* fundraising money."

"Of course I want to win, but isn't it wrong for us not to give the check back?"

John considered Bart's reaction for a moment. "Bart, we're doing Kyle a favor by returning him his money, right?"

113

"Yeah, sure."

"If you *really* think about it, the money from the check isn't even Kyle's. That's money for spaghetti dinners. And anyway, it's not *our* fault that he lost his money. Kyle should be thankful to get *any* of his money back."

John's plan was starting to sound better to Bart. "Okay, so you're saying that Kyle gets *all* of his own money back, but we hide the check. Let's do it."

John quickly hid the check and they hurried on to class.

Later in the day

Miss Paulette's class returned from their lunch break. For some reason, John had eaten very little. He'd left most of his sandwich on his plate, and he didn't even touch his dessert. That was certainly not like him. He was known for demanding second helpings. Now he sat quietly at his desk, wishing to be left alone. As he stared outside of the classroom window, he slowly began to realize what was wrong. His conscience was bothering him. *I shouldn't have hidden Kyle's check. If my class wins the contest because I was dishonest, I'll feel horrible. I won't even be able to enjoy the pizza party or the trip to the lake because I lied and cheated.* John squirmed uncomfortably at his desk, trying to decide what to do. After many moments of going back and forth with the issue, he chose to make things right. He decided to tell Miss Paulette the location of Kyle's missing check.

Ask Yourself...

1. If you had seen Kyle's money on the floor, what would you have done?

2. When someone lies to you, is it hard to fully trust them again?

3. If people don't trust you, is it more difficult for you to make friends? Explain.

Last Word

Our story's verse illustrates that it's important to God that we are always honest. He favorably views honesty and fairness while He frowns on lying, cheating, and stealing. John was guilty of cheating in the fundraising competition *and* lying about his friend's check. He felt terrible as he considered his dishonest behavior. At the end of our story, John felt bad and realized that he should tell his teacher that he had hidden Kyle's check. Shame and embarrassment made it very difficult to do so.

Our story's verse speaks of 'differing weights' and 'dishonest scales.'" You may wonder what that means. It refers to a dishonest practice by store owners that was common many years ago. A store owner's scales weighed items that they were selling such as fruits and vegetables. In order for the store owner to make more money, the scales were set incorrectly (making items appear to weigh more than they actually did). This allowed merchants to cheat their customers and charge them more money. Of course, this was not pleasing to God.

It's almost impossible for a dishonest person to find *true* happiness in life. Once a person is dishonest, they typically have to spend much of their time telling more and more fibs just to cover up the lies that they earlier told. That's not much fun! People who choose to be dishonest are seldom trusted by others, making it difficult for them to have healthy relationships. This includes relationships with family members, friends, and teachers. More important, dishonest people struggle to have a good relationship with the One that matters most—God. Without Him, one is destined to experience a great deal of disappointment and emptiness inside. Make the right choice: honesty.

Chapter Fifteen

HANDLING CONFLICT WITH OTHERS

Verse: Now Lot, who was moving about with Abram, also had flocks and herds and tents. But the land could not support them while they stayed together, for their possessions were so great they were not able to stay together. And quarreling arose between Abram's herdsmen and the herdsmen of Lot. So Abram said to Lot, "Let's not have any quarrelling between you and me, or between your herdsmen and mine, for we are brothers. Is not the whole land before you? Let's part company. If you go to the left, I'll go to the right; if you go to the right, I'll go to the left."

Genesis 13: 5-9

Too Many Tigers

"All right students, please return to your desks. Snack time is over," said Miss Pugh as she brought her class to order. As the children found their seats, she stepped forward. "I'm about to place an index card face down on each of your desks. Don't touch your card until I give further instruction."

Miss Pugh smiled to herself as she watched the student's curious faces while she passed out the cards. She took pride in seeing them display interest in her classroom activities. She returned to the front of the room. "As you all know, it's time for us to get started on our science projects. Each of you will be working in groups of four. The card on your desk will reveal which group you'll be a part of. You'll be in one of the following—the 'snake group,' the 'bird group,' the 'fish group,' or the 'big cat group.'"

Many students excitedly voiced their wishes aloud.

"I want to be in the snake group!" said Ronnie.

"I hope I'm in the bird group," said Deronda.

Many other students chimed in as Miss Pugh looked on, smiling. She loved seeing her students enthused about their schoolwork. After soaking in a few more moments of excitement, she spoke again. "Attention, everyone. It's now the time you've all been waiting for. Turn over your cards and find your project partners!"

A mad scramble ensued as children scurried about the room searching for classmates with matching cards. Due to the chaos, Miss Pugh assisted students in finding their partners. Once this was accomplished, she directed each group to their project table. Miss Pugh was now nearly out of breath. "Guys, it's time for me to give you directions, so listen closely." She took a deep breath. "I'm asking each of you to write a two-page report for me, and I want a lot of variety within each group. For example, if you are a member of the 'fish group,' each of you must choose a *different* type of fish to write about. Also, you must all work together as a team to design and decorate a poster board. Any questions?"

"I have one," said Ron. "Why do we have to work as a team? Why can't we just do it on our own?"

Miss Pugh had heard that question many times before. "In my class, I want you all to have opportunities to improve your ability to work together as a team. As you get older, you'll see that teamwork is an extremely important skill to have. Anything else?"

No one spoke. With the remaining class time, Miss Pugh allowed time on the computers for students to get ideas for their project.

The next day, each of the four groups worked on their projects. The 'snake group' and 'fish group' performed well together because project partners helped each other and displayed teamwork. The 'big cat' and 'bird' groups were a different story.

Big Cat Group

"The first thing we've got to decide is what each of us will write about," said Gaysha. "I was thinking about doing my report on leopards. Their spotted fur makes them the prettiest cat."

Fred nodded. "Fine with me, because I'm writing about lions, kings of the jungle."

Shane shrugged. "Well, you can write about lions if you want, but I'm doing mine on the coolest cat of all, the tiger."

"Who says *you're* doing your report on tigers?" asked Pieri. "I'm writing *my* report on tigers. Tigers are the name of my favorite football team."

Shane laughed. "That's a dumb reason to pick tigers. Anyway, I picked it first!"

Pieri was now annoyed. "It doesn't matter who picked it first. And my reason for choosing tigers is just as good as yours."

Gaysha cut in. "One of you needs to pick something else to write about. Remember, Miss Pugh said that our grade depends on how well we can work together."

"I'm not picking anything else!" said Shane.

Pieri glared at him. "Me either!"

The two boys continued to argue. Neither was willing to give an inch. This caught Miss Pugh's attention.

Disappointed that they could not come to terms, she approached their table to resolve the matter.

Bird Group

"All right, we need to decide what we're writing about," Heather said to her project partners.

"I want to write about eagles," Raymond quickly responded.

"I think I'll write my report on falcons," said Brad. "I watched a cool show about them with my brother last week. Did you know that they can actually see something as small as a mouse over a mile away?"

Heather looked over at Lauren. "Lauren, you're awfully quiet. What bird do you want to write about?"

Lauren smiled. "Flamingos. I've always loved watching them at the zoo."

Heather's heart sank with Lauren's words. Heather had been excited to learn that she was a member of the 'bird group' because flamingos were her favorite of all wildlife. It was only a week ago that she had commented to her mother that they were "the most beautiful bird of all." Now she feared that she might have to change her plans. Her only chance was to persuade Lauren to choose another topic. "Lauren, I really want to write *my* report on flamingos. Could you please choose something else to write about?"

Lauren stood firm. "No, I really want to write about flamingos. My mom and I like them so much that we have our own special flamingo collection at home, over a hundred items."

Heather sighed. "Then aren't you just a little tired of them?"

"Oh, no. They're my favorite."

Heather was running out of ideas. *I could insist on writing my report on flamingos. After all, I have a right to choose flamingos just as much as Lauren does.* Then another thought came to Heather. She recalled last week's lesson at church. It was about treating people as you would like to be treated. She then realized what she needed to do. "Lauren, because you know so much about flamingos, I bet that you'll be able to write a great paper on them. I'll write mine on owls instead. After all, aren't they the wisest bird?"

Both girls laughed as they alerted Miss Pugh that each group member had chosen a topic. Their teacher was happy to learn that the team had avoided a conflict and was able to work things out.

Ask Yourself...

1. Based on how each team worked together, which one do you think received the poorest grade?

2. What do you think Miss Pugh meant when she said "As you get older, you'll see that teamwork is an extremely valuable skill to have"?

3. Think of someone that you have trouble getting along with at school. What is something that *you* can do to help avoid problems with them?

Last Word

In our story, Miss Pugh tested her student's abilities to work together. She wanted group members to help each other and solve problems as they arose. The 'big cat group' proved to be the only group that failed to meet her expectation. This was because Shane and Pieri made no effort to work out their conflict. Due to this, the "big cat group" undoubtedly received a poor grade. The "bird group" faced a similar problem when both Heather and Lauren aspired to write about flamingos. Fortunately, Heather recalled a previous lesson from church and decided to place Lauren's wishes above her own. Because she chose to do this, her group avoided a bad grade. Heather's actions were honorable, much like Abram's in our story's scripture. Although Jewish law gave Abram the right to choose the land that he wished to settle, he allowed Lot to make the choice instead. Abram's actions were honorable because he put Lot's wishes ahead of his own. Due to this, they were able to avoid conflict.

It's very important that you make efforts to avoid problems with others and display teamwork. If you learn how to avoid conflicts, you greatly improve your ability to be successful in life. This skill will assist you in making friends, having an enjoyable family life, prospering at work, and most importantly, pleasing God.

Chapter Sixteen

TURNING TO GOD WHEN AFRAID

Verse: Do not be afraid, Abram. I am your **shield,** your very great reward.

Genesis 15:1

Stage Fright

Each day after school, Seth's mother reviewed the contents of her son's backpack. She typically found homework assignments, returned paperwork, and occasionally a note from his teacher. Reviewing these items helped her to prepare for their "study time" together each evening. On this particular afternoon, a note from Seth's teacher caught her attention. She was surprised to see that Seth was assigned to give a ten minute presentation to his class on Thursday. She found it strange that he hadn't mentioned it since there were only three days remaining to prepare. *Time is running out. I'll have to get down to the bottom of this as soon as he returns from his karate lesson.*

Seth and his father returned home. He could not contain his excitement as he raced through the front door to tell his mother about practice.

"Hey, Mom, you aren't going to believe what Master Blake did in Karate class today. He broke a big stack of boards with his bare hands. It was awesome!"

Seth's mother smiled as he shared *every* detail of his karate lesson. His recollection of practice went on and on. Finally, after much time had passed, he winded down. The moment had come for his mother to ask about the upcoming assignment.

"It sounds like you had a great time at practice today." She paused for a second before changing the subject. "Hey, I have something I need to ask you. I was going through your backpack this afternoon and noticed that Miss Reifeiss has asked you to speak in front of your class on Thursday. I was wondering why you haven't mentioned it. I can help you prepare."

Before his mother could continue, she could clearly see that something was wrong. Seth no longer appeared bright-eyed with a big grin across his face. His smile transformed to a frown as he looked away to stare down at the kitchen floor. "I, uh, don't know," he nervously replied. "I guess I was going to tell you soon."

Due to Seth's obvious discomfort, she decided not to press the issue any further for the moment. She simply smiled and said, "Well, Miss Reifeiss said that you need to decide on a topic to teach your classmates for ten minutes. So try to think of something that you'll enjoy talking to them about. And don't worry, we'll have you ready to present in no time."

Seth slowly looked up. "Okay," he mumbled and quietly left the kitchen. Seth's mother had never seen him act quite like that before. It was apparent that he didn't care for this particular assignment. As she prepared dinner, she considered various ways to help him become more enthused about the project.

Later that evening

As Seth's mother entered his bedroom to tell him good-night, she decided to further discuss the assignment. She

126

pulled up a chair next to his bed. "Your assignment sounds like fun. Have you decided what you would like to teach?"

Once again, Seth looked away. "I don't know. I haven't really wanted to think about it."

"You haven't wanted to think about it? Why is that?"

There was a long pause before Seth spoke. It was difficult for him to express his true feelings. "Well, uh, to me it, uh, looks like being a teacher is a hard job, even for grown-ups like Miss Reifeiss. And I'm *just a kid*. How can *I* do it right? I guess I'm just scared that I'll mess up."

Seth's mother carefully chose her words before replying. She patted him on the shoulder. "It's natural to sometimes feel afraid, especially when you're doing something that you've never done before. Everyone experiences fear from time to time, *even Dad and I*."

Seth appeared shocked. "You mean to tell me that Dad is sometimes afraid. I don't believe that."

"Believe it or not, everyone has fears, *even* Dad. Do you know what helps me when I'm afraid?"

Seth shrugged his shoulders, waiting for his mother's response.

"I pray to God for strength and remember that He is always with me."

Seth considered her words. After a few seconds, he smiled. "That sounds like a good idea. So you're saying that if can I remember that God is with me while I'm in front of the class, it'll be easier?"

"That's right. It's important to always be aware of God's presence. He wants you to ask for His help."

Before she could continue, Seth interrupted. "I've got a great idea! I'm going to get Grandpa Barry to help me with a lesson on farming. I can show the class pictures of the farm equipment that he uses and talk about what he plants in his fields."

His mother breathed a sigh of relief, believing that

he may be over his classroom jitters. "You can even take samples of soybean, corn, and wheat to show the class. I bet they would like that."

After listening to all of his big plans, she kissed him goodnight and left his bedroom. She smiled to herself, realizing that God was active in her child's life.

Ask Yourself...

1. Before hearing the story, did you realize that *everyone* experiences fear at some time, even adults?

2. Can you remember a time when you were afraid? If yes, explain how you handled the situation.

3. Have you ever prayed when you were scared?

Last Word

It can be said that one's life is made up of a multitude of unique events that occur on a daily basis. Not one day is quite the same. Many of these events are welcomed by us in a positive manner, while others may be scary or uncomfortable. In our story, just such an "event" occurs in Seth's life. His teacher instructed him to lead a class presentation, and he becomes afraid. Seth is unsure as to whether he can perform this particular task in a satisfactory manner. Many of us react similarly to Seth when faced with uncertainty in our life. When Seth's mother helps him to understand that praying to God provides strength and comfort, he's able to move forward and face his fears. Having an understanding of our story's verse can provide *you* the same comfort and strength that Seth enjoyed. The verse shows us that God acts as our shield, meaning He is protecting us. Don't hesitate to pray to God when you're afraid. Remember, you don't have to face your problems alone!

Chapter Seventeen

BEING MODEST

Verse: Joseph had a dream, and when he told it to his brothers, they hated him all the more. He said to them, "Listen to this dream I had: We were binding sheaves of grain out in the field when suddenly my sheaf rose and stood upright, while your sheaves gathered around mine and bowed down to it. His brothers said to him, "Do you intend to reign over us? Will you actually rule us?" And they hated him all the more because of his dream and what he said. Then he had another dream, and he told it to his brothers. "Listen," he said, "I had another dream, and this time the sun and moon and eleven stars were bowing down to me." When he told his father as well as his brothers, his father rebuked him and said, "What is this dream you had? Will your mother and I and your brothers actually come and bow down to the ground before you?" His brothers were jealous of him, but his father kept the matter in mind.

Genesis 37: 5-11

The Grass Is Always Greener on *My* Side

Christa, Adrianna, and Karlee were always the first students to arrive for Miss Scroggins' morning class. Each girl's parents had jobs that required an early start, so they usually had the classroom to themselves. Miss Scroggins allowed them to use the computers or play board games at Christa's table as they waited for other students to arrive. Miss Scroggins always kept a close eye on them since their time together often resulted in conflict. This particular morning was no different.

Christa walked up. "Hello, girls. Sorry I'm late this morning. It took me a while to find my new shoes that I wanted to show off. How do you like them?"

Karlee looked up from a puzzle that she was putting together. "Oh, hi, Christa." She glanced down. "Your shoes look nice."

Christa frowned. "Nice? Is that the best that you can do?" She looked over at Adrianna. "Surely *you* can appreciate these shoes." She lowered her tone to a whisper. "They're very expensive. Not everyone can afford shoes like these."

Adrianna exhibited very little emotion. "I guess not."

Christa walked over to Adrianna's desk. "What're you reading?"

Adrianna smiled. "It's a book that teaches how to play the piano. I'm thinking about giving it a try."

Christa laughed. "You'll never learn how to play the piano by reading a book. You need private lessons like the ones I get. My mom said that I can have lessons to learn the piano, gymnastics, or whatever I choose. And I don't have to tell you that I'm already great with the violin after just three months of private lessons. My parents are the best!"

It was early in the day, but Adrianna was already growing tired of Christa's bragging. *I'll just do my best to ignore it. I need to stay out of trouble.* She purposely changed the subject. "Karlee, did you find out which softball team you're playing on this year?"

Karlee smiled. "I'm playing for the Rebels, just like last year. Coach Gary called my dad and gave him the news yesterday."

Adrianna appeared shocked. "Are you serious? We're

finally on the same team! We're actually going to be teammates!"

"That's great!" said Karlee. "This is gonna be our best season."

As Adrianna and Karlee excitedly continued their discussion, Christa quietly looked on. She was feeling left out. Karlee noticed this and tried to include her. "Christa, I bet you'll be glad when the season starts. It's really cool how your team gets to travel all over the state and even stay in hotel rooms. Our team only plays here in the city."

Karlee's efforts to include Christa in the conversation seemed to backfire, mainly because Christa had always been jealous that Karlee and Adrianna were such good friends. Christa was not happy. "The reason that we travel all over the state is because there aren't any good teams to play around here. Coach Jamie told us that we were all specially picked to play for the Heat because we're the best players in the area. The league that you two play in would be *really* boring for me and my teammates because we wouldn't have any real competition."

Karlee found Christa's words hurtful since she'd only tried to be nice and include her in the conversation. She turned away to hide her tears. Adrianna had a much different reaction. "Christa, anytime you're not the center of attention, you either talk bad about people or you have to start bragging on yourself!" Adrianna spoke loudly enough to alert Miss Scroggins. The teacher had seen this behavior so many times that she realized an intervention was necessary to ensure that things didn't get out of hand.

"All right girls, if you can't get along, it's time to go back to your own table. You can spend the rest of your free time sitting alone thinking about how to improve your conduct." The girls quickly gathered their belongings and moved to their seats. The three sat quietly and considered their behaviors as they waited for class to begin.

The next morning

Christa arrived early as usual. As she entered the classroom, she could see that Karlee and Adrianna were already playing on the computer. She approached the girls. "What're you playing?"

Adrianna glanced in her direction. "Oh, nothing much." Adrianna's attention shifted back to the computer screen.

"Can I play?" asked Christa.

"Sure you can," replied Adrianna.

But instead of allowing Christa to join in their game, Adrianna and Karlee got up from their chairs and left Christa alone with the computer. She sat down and stared blankly at the computer screen. As Christa thought about their reaction, she began to consider her own behavior from the previous morning. It slowly became clear to her why Karlee and Adrianna continued to be angry. She began to feel sad, realizing that all of her bragging and putting others down had finally caught up with her. Christa knew it was time to make some changes.

Ask Yourself...

1. Identify a time that that you saw someone brag. How did it make you feel?

2. Do you ever brag? Explain why.

3. How can bragging make it more difficult to have friends?

Last Word

Have you ever heard the old saying, "Actions speak louder than words"? There is a lot of truth to this statement. Your actions are typically how others learn what type of person you truly are. Often, people who are boastful and brag on themselves don't back up their words with actions. "Talk" has very little meaning when action doesn't back it up.

The verse from our story demonstrates how bragging can be harmful. Joseph's bragging and boastful manner resulted in his father's disapproval and his brothers hating him. Seldom does *any* good come from bringing extra attention to yourself. It can actually do more harm than good. For instance, exhibiting a boastful nature may result in having poor relationships or even a lack of relationships in your life. Don't be like Christa in our story. If you feel like bragging, choose to brag on someone besides yourself. God will be pleased as you make someone feel good.

Chapter Eighteen

FOLLOWING RULES

Verse: To do what is right and just is more acceptable to the Lord than sacrifice.

Proverbs 21:2-3

Freedom at Last

Unlike most Monday mornings, there was a buzz of excitement among the students. What made this particular Monday different was the soon-to-be arrival of the new class pet. This was the only topic of discussion as children filed into the classroom. Blaine, sitting near the back of the room, peered over students that blocked his view of the doorway. He hoped to be the first to catch a glimpse of Miss Germany and the class pet. All of their imaginations ran wild as they speculated about what type of pet it would be.

"I bet it's a rabbit," said Blaine. "That's what Miss Ridings's class has."

"Nah, I don't think Miss Germany will copy another class," replied his best friend, Chandler. "It'll probably be something awesome like a giant spider."

"It better not be!" shrieked Sarah in disgust. "It'll be something that both the boys *and* girls will like."

The two boys laughed as they continued to focus on the

doorway. At that very moment, Miss Germany entered the classroom. She was pushing a cart covered by a purple and gold colored tablecloth. She smiled as children jumped from their seats and surrounded her. "I know you're all looking forward to meeting our new class pet, but first let me say that I'm so proud of each of you. The class really deserves this reward. You've all worked hard on your assignments, and your conduct has greatly improved. So without further delay, meet the newest member of our class!" Miss Germany took one end of the tablecloth and quickly jerked it away as a magician might. A glass terrarium held their reward, a Leopard Gecko.

Blaine could be heard over all of his classmates. "That's the coolest lizard I've ever seen! Look how big it is. I've never seen one like that before."

Sarah smiled. "I like its yellow body and black spots. It's actually kind of pretty for a lizard."

For several minutes, the gecko had their full attention. Children hovered over the terrarium and asked question after question, ranging from where geckos could be found in the wild to what they like to eat. Miss Germany enjoyed her students' interest in the gecko and hoped that they would learn from the discussion.

"Leopard Geckos live in Central Asia. They usually grow to be six to nine inches long. This particular one is two years old and is already full-grown." Miss Germany went on to discuss the gecko's eating habits as well as each student's responsibilities in caring for their new friend. They were all eager to get started.

Several weeks passed as the children took turns feeding the gecko, filling his water tray, and making sure his home was clean. They enjoyed their pet, but as time passed, their focus was divided among many other interests and school activities. The gecko was no longer the center of attention until Blaine came up with an idea. As he poured fresh water into the gecko's dish, he looked slyly over at Chandler. "Hey, don't you think it's been kind of boring just watching Rex sitting here, trapped in this terrarium?" Blaine lowered his voice. "What do you say we take him to the playground with us?"

Chandler stared at Blaine for a moment, trying to decide if he was truly serious. Finally, he responded. "I think it might be a really bad idea. Don't you remember the most important rule that Miss Germany gave us? She said that we're to *never* take Rex from his home."

Blaine was prepared with a response. "Yeah, I know it's against the rules, but Miss Germany will never know we did it. I promise you that we won't get caught. I'll just hide Rex here in my jacket." Blaine studied Chandler, who now seemed to be seriously considering the plan. "Don't just think about us. Think about Rex. He's cooped up in this box every single day. How would that make *you* feel?"

The idea began to sound good to Chandler, even though he knew it was against the rules. He flashed a smile at Blaine. "Let's do it."

Blaine's heart raced as he carefully grasped the gecko and slowly raised him out of his terrarium. Chandler stood guard at the doorway, making sure they wouldn't get caught in the act. Blaine tucked Rex into his pocket and they headed for the playground."Hey, let's take Rex behind the big tree. No one will see us there."

Chandler surveyed the playground, looking in each direction. "Good idea."

The two boys enjoyed the gecko since they had it all to themselves for a change. They took turns holding and petting him. Before long, they lost track of everything going on around them and jumped when Sarah suddenly appeared.

She couldn't believe her eyes. "You two are going to be in *so* much trouble! I can't believe you took him out of the classroom!"

Blaine knew he had to act fast since Sarah had reported his wrong-doings many times before. He would do just about anything to avoid another visit to Principal Bailey's office. "Sarah, would you like to hold Rex?" Blaine used the nicest tone he could muster. "Wouldn't it be neat to be the only girl in the entire school to hold him? It can be our little secret."

Sarah was hesitant. She knew that breaking the rules with Blaine and Chandler was a bad idea, but she had often wondered what it would be like to hold the gecko. She quickly scanned the playground, making sure that no one was watching. Her classmates appeared to be busy with other activities. She made her decision. Sarah turned to Blaine. "Give him to me."

Blaine obliged her before she had a chance to change her mind. He quickly handed off the gecko. Sarah winced as the gecko's scaly body touched her hands. Rex quickly began to squirm in her hands, which was just too much for Sarah. She threw her arms up in the air and screamed. The gecko dropped to the ground and raced for freedom. In seconds, their teacher and all of their classmates came running to find out what was wrong. The gecko scampered through the playground fence into thick brush and was never seen again.

Ask Yourself...

1. What do you think happened to Blaine, Chandler, and Sarah because they didn't do what was right?

2. Blaine, Chandler, and Sarah were responsible for losing the class pet. How do you believe their classmates felt about them?

3. Think of a time that you were caught breaking a rule. How did it make you feel?

Last Word

Our story's verse focuses on pleasing God through making the choice to do what is right. God wants you to obey rules and avoid wrong doing on a regular basis. In our story, Blaine, Chandler, and Sarah make a poor choice. They knew that taking the gecko out of the terrarium was wrong, but their own desires were more important to them than doing the right thing. They did not understand the importance of the rule set by Miss Germany until after the gecko had escaped. By then it was too late. In choosing to break a rule, they suffered in many ways. First, they would never see their pet again. Second, they faced punishment from their teacher and the principal. Last but not least, they had to face anger and disappointment from their classmates. If they had just chosen to follow the rules, they would've avoided all of these unpleasant consequences. Our story is a good example of why it's important to follow rules and do what you know is right. Remember, it will please God and make life more enjoyable for all.

Chapter Nineteen

SHARING

Verse: They devoted themselves to the apostles' teaching and to the fellowship, to the breaking of bread and to prayer. Everyone was filled with awe, and many wonders and miraculous signs were done by the apostles. All the believers were together and had everything in common. Selling their possessions and goods, **they gave to anyone as he had need**. Every day they continued to meet together in the temple courts. They broke bread in their homes and ate together with glad and sincere hearts, praising God and enjoying the favor of all people. And the Lord added to their number daily those who were being saved.

Acts 2:42-47

Three's Company?

Robert could barely focus on his schoolwork as he eyed the clock hanging over Mr. Windham's desk. Robert knew that he had given the clock far more attention than he'd given his teacher as he wrapped up his discussion on fossils. He knew that he should be listening, but he simply couldn't help himself. All he could think about was how much fun he had with Dallas during the last recess, playing catch with the classroom football. Minutes felt like hours for Robert as he continued to stare at the clock. After what seemed like forever, Mr. Windham completed the lesson and announced that it was time for afternoon recess. As always, he reminded the children to obey the playground rules. As they all made their way down the hallway towards the playground, Dallas grabbed the football from the classroom supply closet. The two boys were ready to play.

Once outside, they began tossing the ball back and forth. They stood close together as they threw the ball and gradually moved farther apart with each catch. Of course, this made the game more challenging. The farther they moved apart, the more they laughed and rooted each other on. They cheered loudly, showing more excitement with each catch. They were so involved in their game that they didn't notice that the new boy was watching them. He timidly approached Robert and Dallas.

"Hey, can I play?" he asked.

At that very moment, Robert happened to drop a pass. Robert angrily turned to the boy. "Look what you made me do! I was catching the ball just fine until you showed up. Now we have to start all over. Thanks a lot."

The boy's eyes widened with surprise. "I didn't make you miss it. I wasn't even close to you."

Dallas glared at him. "You *did* make him miss it. He caught every ball before *you* showed up. Just go away."

The boy couldn't believe his ears. He looked Dallas straight in the face. "You know, that football isn't even yours. It belongs to the whole class. Everyone has the right to play with it."

Robert shook his head. "Everyone knows that Dallas and I play with this ball *every* recess."

Dallas agreed. "As far as I'm concerned, that makes the ball ours."

"Have you ever heard of sharing? I've always shared my things with other kids. It's what you're supposed to do."

Robert stepped towards the new boy. "We don't have to

share if we don't want to. We had the ball first, and we plan to keep it."

"You two aren't very nice. I don't even want to play with you anymore, but I'm still going to tell Mr. Windham about this. Then you'll both be sorry." Obviously hurt, he walked away, shoulders slumped. *I only wanted a chance to make some new friends.* He returned to the spot where he'd been standing earlier. Feeling lonely, he watched the others play.

Robert and Dallas continued their game as if nothing had happened. The remaining moments of recess didn't seem as much fun for Robert. Instead of focusing on the game, his mind was elsewhere. *I wonder how mad Mr. Windham's gonna be with us for not sharing. When he hears about it, we'll probably be stuck with classroom chores instead of going to recess. I should have just let him play with us. What was I thinking?*

Ask Yourself...

1   How did the boys' behavior hurt *everyone* involved in the story?

2. Do you consider yourself to be one who regularly shares with others?

3. How can sharing benefit you?

Last Word

Our story's verse is an excellent example of how good things come from sharing with others. The people that are mentioned in the verse are actually selling their own possessions in order to make money to help those who have very little. *Now that's sharing!* Of course, at school you'll never be asked to give your money and possessions to other students. Our scripture shows that those willing to share will receive blessings from God. What He would like to see is for you to share and avoid selfishness, showing a caring attitude for others. It may improve your ability to make friends and avoid conflict. It will not only bring happiness to those you share with...it will give you a great feeling inside. Make a point to share the things that God has provided you. Start today!

Chapter Twenty

Asking God for Forgiveness

Verse: The Lord is compassionate and gracious, slow to anger, abounding in love. He will not always accuse, nor will he harbor his anger forever. He does not treat us as our sins deserve or repay us according to our iniquities. For as high as the heavens are above the earth, so great is his love for those who fear him; as far as the east is from the west, so far has he removed our transgressions from us. As a father has compassion on his children, so the Lord has compassion for those who fear him for he knows how we are formed. He remembers that we are dust.

Psalms 103: 8-14

I'm Not Worthy

Norma, deep in thought, was walking home after a long day of school. Her pace slowed with each step as she considered what awaited her. Norma's pulse quickened when her home came into view just a few blocks down the street. She paused on the sidewalk and considered her options. Her stomach tightened as she envisioned herself face-to-face with her parents. *I'm not ready for that. I need a plan.*

She quickly veered from the sidewalk, opting for a little-known path into a wooded area that her older brother had once shown her. She felt a sense of relief as she made her way down the winding trail, taking her farther from home. In the back of Norma's mind, she realized that this relief was only temporary, for she had to return home sooner or later.

After walking for a few minutes, she came upon a small pond. As Norma approached, she slung her backpack onto the ground and found a place to sit that overlooked the water. Norma welcomed the quietness of the forest and took in her surroundings. All she could hear was a chorus of crickets. She spotted a mother duck swimming with her young on the far side of the pond.

"I wish I were a duck. Life would be so much simpler." She watched them a moment longer before returning to her problems. Norma reached into her backpack and pulled out her report card. She shook her head in disgust as she reviewed her grades. Unfortunately, there were more C's, D's and F's than A's and B's. "How did I let this happen? And how can I face my parents? I can't go home with this."

Norma imagined her parents' reactions and began to consider a variety of excuses for her poor performance. How could her mom and dad possibly expect her to make good grades with all of the extra chores given to her since Doug was born? *I don't even have time for homework.* Norma believed that all of her parents' time and energy was spent on Doug. *It's all about the baby now. Everything was fine before he was born.* And to top things off, her parents were constantly arguing. *How can I be expected to focus on school with that going on?*

For a moment or two, Norma made herself believe that her bad grades were justified. But as she sorted out her thoughts, feelings of doubt and disappointment slowly returned. This made her consider much more than just her report card.

"It's not just my grades. When Mom and Dad attend parent-teacher conference, they'll hear enough to ground me forever." Over the past two weeks, she'd been in trouble for talking back to the teachers, fighting with students, cheating on a test, and cursing. *"What have I become?"*

Staring over the water, Norma began to realize that she had fallen victim to peer pressure. Her new friends constantly dared her to break school rules, and for some crazy reason, she did exactly what they told her to do. Was it really so important to please them? She hardly ever thought for herself anymore.

Sadness flooded over Norma as she considered her recent behaviors. "I don't have any *real* friends. My parents and teachers aren't happy with me, and I never seem to make the right choices. Is there any hope for me?"

Norma felt overwhelmed. She had a multitude of problems and knew that it was time to make changes in her life . . . but she had no idea where to start. She glanced down at her backpack and noticed that one of her textbooks had slipped out—her religion book. Without thought, Norma opened the book instead of stuffing it back into the bag. A Bible verse in bold print caught her eye.

The Lord is compassionate and gracious, slow to anger, abounding in love. He will not always accuse, nor will he harbor his anger forever. He does not treat us as our sins deserve or repay us according to our iniquities. For as high as the heavens are above the earth, so great is his love for those who fear him; as far as the east is from the west, so far has he removed our transgressions from us. As a father has compassion on his children, so the Lord has compassion for those who fear him for he knows how we are formed. He remembers that we are dust.

As Norma finished reading, she wiped away a tear. "How can God forgive me when I've ignored Him for so long?

After all I've done to hurt myself and others, why would I even be worth God's attention?"

Moments earlier, Norma had no idea how to turn her life around and find even a glimpse of happiness. Now, the solution was crystal clear. "It's been a long time since God's been important to me. That's going to change, starting right now." Norma leaned back against her backpack and closed her eyes. She prayed aloud.

"God, thank you so much for still caring about me and showing forgiveness for all of the bad things I've done. I know I don't deserve your forgiveness, but I'm asking for it. I promise that from now on, I'll do my best to make decisions that please you. I'll show respect for my parents and teachers. I'll choose friends that don't want to change me and like me for the unique person that you created.

"God, give me strength as I face my current problems. I'm not asking that you rescue me. I know that I deserve discipline for some of my actions. Just help me as I make changes in my life, and please allow others to see that I'm doing my best to live a life that is pleasing to You. Be near me as I head home. In His name, amen."

Norma stood up. The sun was now fading behind the trees, causing her surroundings to grow dim. *I'd better get home before Mom and Dad start worrying.*

Without hesitation, Norma strapped on her backpack and headed back into the world. Unlike earlier in the day, she now walked with confidence and hope. From that point on, Norma vowed to place God first in her life.

Ask Yourself

1. Norma believes that she's not deserving of God's forgiveness. Is anyone truly worthy of God's forgiveness?

2. Norma's relationship with God suffered due to her inability to resist peer pressure. What factors negatively impact your relationship with God?

3. What do you need to ask God's forgiveness for at this time?

Last Word

In our story, Norma strayed from God, which resulted in numerous negative behaviors. These included disrespecting teachers, fighting with students, cheating on tests, and cursing. Over time, Norma developed a negative perception of herself, which resulted in low self-esteem and a distant relationship with God. She did not feel worthy of forgiveness from anyone, especially God. The truth is that *no* human being is worthy of God's forgiveness. Not one of us. We're very fortunate that God chooses to forgive us for our sins. Concerning His forgiveness, Norma was surprised that all she had to do was ask for it. Of course, she had to ask in a sincere and regretful manner. She couldn't be granted forgiveness if she asked half-heartedly, intending to repeat her negative behaviors.

Great benefits come from receiving God's forgiveness. His forgiveness provides us an opportunity to move away from past mistakes and establish a more meaningful, Christ-like existence. His forgiveness offers us a "clean slate" with feelings of peace as opposed to a life of turmoil and unrest. When God forgives, it's as if our past sins never occurred. Have you ever heard the saying "forgive and forget"?

Although we may forgive, it may be extremely difficult to forget. God forgives us completely!

Norma's downfall was giving in to peer pressure. It distanced her from God. Ultimately, she disliked what she'd become and knew she had to change. She redeemed herself with an excellent decision (asking for forgiveness) after a lot of poor choices. Although Norma realized that she wasn't worthy of forgiveness, she asked anyway. Her request was granted, and Norma's life began moving in the right direction. If your life resembles Norma's in any way, make the same choice that she did. Ask God to forgive you of your sins. A greater life is awaiting you. Ask for His forgiveness right now.

CPSIA information can be obtained at www.ICGtesting.com
Printed in the USA
LVOW040945051112

305875LV00001B/6/P

9 781619 960299